SCHOLASTIC

D1586095

The **BIG** Book of
Differentiated
READING
RESPONSE
Activities

75 Engaging, Tiered Reproducibles to Help You Find
the Just-Right Activity for Every Reader

by Rhonda Graff

New York ○ Toronto ○ London ○ Auckland ○ Sydney
New Delhi ○ Mexico City ○ Hong Kong ○ Buenos Aires

Teaching *Resources*

Dedicated to my mother and father
with love and appreciation.

With special thanks to Liza Charlesworth,
Jaime Lucero, and Gina Shaw.
Thank you to Holly S., Linda B., Brianna S.,
and Steve S. for your input and feedback.
Love to Craig and Daniel.

-- R. G.

Edited by Gina Shaw
Cover design by Scott Davis
Interior design by Grafica
Illustrations by Maxie Chambliss, Kelly Kennedy, Debbie Schultz,
Margaret Wong, and Jaime Lucero
ISBN: 978-0-545-55233-2

Contents

Introduction

What Will This Book Do for YOU?

It will make your teaching life easier!

Teachers differentiate all day long. We are always assessing our students and making adaptations and changes that allow us to better reach each child. We change assignment requirements, give extra time, level texts, scaffold projects, and provide alternatives. We group our students and regroup our students. We assess, change instruction, and look for new and interesting ways to deliver curriculum. Children are not all alike. The demographics have changed in our schools and our classes include a very diverse range of learners. Teachers must recognize the importance of understanding each child's needs in order to create a successful learning environment.

Children (and adults) learn differently. Not every adult could be a surgeon or an electrician because our inherent differences make us strong in different ways. Without these differences, this world would be rather dull. Children do not have a choice whether or not to go to school. Many students' strengths are life strengths, not classroom strengths. Our students come to our classrooms ready to learn, but they are not always successful. No child comes to school wanting to fail. Our job as teachers is to recognize these differences, whether they are learning-based, physical, emotional, or cultural, and to create the proper learning environment to foster success.

Children can be flexibly grouped for different tasks and reasons. In my class, one student struggled with decoding and spelling, but her comprehension was strong. So, she worked with me in controlled readers to practice her decoding skills and fluency, but she joined my more advanced students for book discussions because she added so much verbally to the group. (Her mother read the book with her at home or a peer read to her so she was able to keep up with both groups.) In this way, her needs were met. She continued to move along in her reading and spelling based on very controlled work, and her comprehension strength was noticed and enhanced by her participation in an advanced group.

Teachers must reassess and change groups as needed. Sometimes students can choose their learning environment; they know if they work better alone, with a partner, or a small group. Differentiation does not mean individualized instruction; it does mean that teachers plan and provide a variety of alternative means of delivery and follow-up work. It means understanding how your students learn best.

Carol Ann Tomlinson has written many books on the topic of differentiation. She refers to four distinct aspects of the curriculum necessary for differentiation: content, process, product, and affect. These elements, in turn, hinge on student readiness, student interest, and student learning profiles. The focus of this book, however, is on "process," specifically, leveled assignments, one small part of differentiation. The intent of this book is not to provide a how-to on all aspects of differentiation.

About This Book

There are many ways to differentiate for your students, but in this book, the main focus is on *leveled activities*. Some of the options for differentiation can be accomplished with little or no advance preparation. However, alternatives such as leveled activities do require advance preparation. Teachers have many responsibilities and designing these alternatives can be time-consuming. In this book, it has been done for you. Each leveled set includes three handouts focusing on the same general concept as noted on the Contents page. There are many more options for differentiation beyond leveled activities, some of which are briefly mentioned in the Appendix.

On Each Teacher Notes Page

On each Teacher Notes page, you'll find:

Pre-assessment Activity Suggestions are provided for a pre-assessment activity. The information from the pre-assessment can be used to help plan instruction and to create appropriate student groups.

Pre-assessments can be used to obtain a general understanding of students' abilities and what supports they need prior to beginning a lesson. Teacher observations, checklists, conversations with the children, and student work (including brief assignments such as webs and lists) all serve as ways to learn more about what your students know and understand. Formal assessments are important too, but are not the only means to understanding your students' abilities. It is important to have good insight into where your students begin, so you can match your instruction accordingly.

Level A, Level B, and Level C Leveled Reproducible Directions For each of the three leveled reproducibles, a brief set of teacher directions is provided. Completed thumbnail sketches of each handout are shown as examples and enlarged thumbnails are included at the back of the book.

Whole-Class Book Chat For each given focus skill, there is a Whole Class Book Chat topic. This is critical to differentiation, because students will move flexibly from group to group (whole class, small group, independent, whole group again). After introducing a topic to a whole class, break students into independent practice, either alone or in small groups, to work on leveled assignments. Then once they finish, regroup the class and use the Whole-Class Book Chat to bring everyone together again. Since the focus of all the handouts is the same, children will have a chance to share their observations and books. This is a great way to encourage reading, as children will be discussing stories, authors, and writing craft.

The Reproducibles

The reproducibles in this book are to be used as reinforcement. Prior to using any of them, the students must be taught the skills. Do not allow students to work on the reproducibles unless you are sure they understand the concepts presented. Some of the activities are cognitively challenging, so be sure your students are prepared for the challenge. The goal is to have the children use these handouts to scaffold

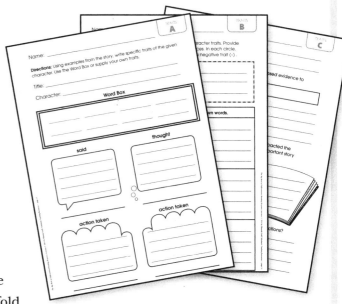

their learning until they no longer need them. With time, the skills will become automatic and students will have an array of reading strategies from which to choose.

Leveled Assignments and Further Suggestions Although there is no one set way to differentiate, teachers need to be cognizant of the range of learners and learning styles in order to pull together options in the classroom. As mentioned, the focus of this book is on "process." Each set includes three leveled handouts focusing on the same general concept.

Many times a teacher will start a lesson with the whole group and then proceed to independent or small-group work. The handouts in this book focus on a range of topics, such as character change over time, setting, theme, and multiple meaning words. The handouts are scaffolded so the children work at their respective levels, building the necessary skills for them to move forward. Always try to keep your students challenged, but successful. These handouts are not a replacement for teaching. The teacher needs to develop and plan the lessons prior to asking the children to complete the handouts. The teacher is involved at all points, recognizing the importance of direct instruction, grouping, monitoring, and assessment (formal and informal). Do not be hard on yourself; recognize that teaching and differentiating are big undertakings.

Remember, these handouts are not meant to be used in isolation. Integrate them into your overall plan and remember to use them flexibly! The goal is for each student to improve from where she or he started.

A Note About Leveled Assignments Leveled assignments are valuable because they allow all the children to focus on a similar lesson with developmentally appropriate materials. The questions that are provided on the handouts encourage students to think concretely and then to move beyond the stated information. The material is challenging for the students at each level. These handouts help reinforce the material taught while promoting independence. The teacher can also use the assignments as an informal assessment and for future planning.

In the Appendix

In the Appendix there is a Student Interest Inventory, a Parent Inventory, a list of Teacher Considerations (questions for teachers to contemplate when planning), and additional projects for your students.

Interest Inventories An important aspect of differentiation is getting to know your students…really well! Teachers may not understand a child beyond the classroom. Using the Student Interest Inventory, students will get a chance to brag a bit about themselves and note some of their struggles. This information is valuable as teachers can draw on student strengths, interests, and weaknesses to better understand and reach their students. Learning what students like (their hobbies and interests) will help in lesson design. As teachers, we are able to adapt lessons so they are more personally meaningful. If you are working with younger students, you may want to read the Student Interest Inventory to them or send it home to be completed with an adult. Also included is a Parent Inventory. This, too, is valuable for learning more about your students and their families.

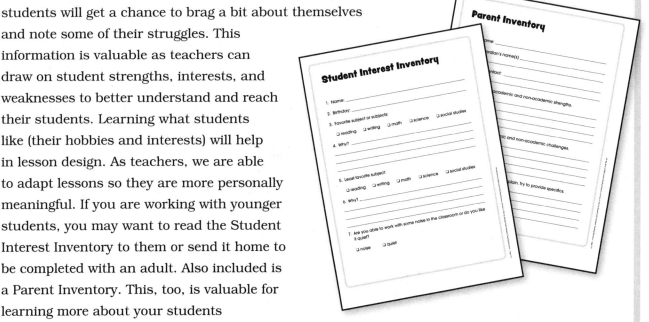

Teacher Considerations
Before you begin to plan a lesson, an assignment, or a unit, this list provides a few helpful things to consider. This list is not exhaustive; however, it will get you thinking a bit outside the box!

Possible Alternative Assignments
There is a section in the Appendix that provides some alternative assignments for students to demonstrate what they learned. These suggestions are project based. They can be completed over time. Expand upon the list as you develop new ways for students to demonstrate learning.

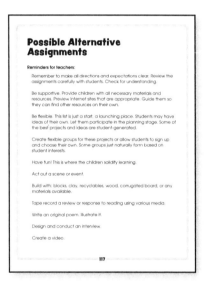

Teacher Considerations

Take some time to consider these questions:

Do students like to work alone, with a partner, in a small group, or in a whole group? Be aware that it is not all or none. Some students are comfortable with multiple grouping formations.

Are your students creative? Would they like to prepare a skit, a song, a movie, or a cartoon to demonstrate their learning? Think beyond a poster.

Are your students ready for abstract material or are they able to handle concrete material more successfully?

Do the students prefer to learn material orally? Do they learn best using visuals? Are they kinesthetic learners?

Do the children have any attention issues?

What type of environment works best for the children?

What talents do the children bring to the task? (musical, artistic, mathematical, socially gifted)

116

Possible Alternative Assignments

Reminders for teachers:

Remember to make all directions and expectations clear. Review the assignments carefully with students. Check for understanding.

Be supportive. Provide children with all necessary materials and resources. Preview Internet sites that are appropriate. Guide them so they can find other resources on their own.

Be flexible. This list is just a start, a launching place. Students may have ideas of their own. Let them participate in the planning stage. Some of the best projects and ideas are student-generated.

Create flexible groups for these projects or allow students to sign up and choose their own. Some groups just naturally form based on student interests.

Have fun! This is where the children solidify learning.

Act out a scene or event.

Build with: blocks, clay, recyclables, wood, corrugated board, or any materials available.

Tape record a review or response to reading using various media.

Write an original poem. Illustrate it.

Design and conduct an interview.

Create a video.

117

Meeting the Common Core State Standards

The tiered activity pages in this book will help you meet your specific state language arts standards as well as those recommended by the Common Core State Standards Initiative (CCSSI). The pages support students in meeting standards in the following strands for grades 2–3: Reading: Foundational Skills, Reading: Literature, Writing, and Language.

The abbreviated standards listed below indicate skills explicitly taught and/or addressed via the activity pages. For more details on the specific standards, go to the CCSSI website at www.corestandards.org.

STRAND	GRADE 2	GRADE 3
Reading: Foundational Skills	RF.2.4 RF.2.4a RF.2.4c	RF.3.4 RF.3.4a RF.3.4c
Reading: Literature	RL.2.1 RL.2.2 RL.2.3 RL.2.5 RL.2.6 RL.2.7 RL.2.9 RL.2.10	RL.3.1 RL.3.2 RL.3.3 RL.3.5 RL.3.6 RL.3.7 RL.3.9 RL.3.10
Writing	W.2.1 W.2.5 W.2.6 W.2.8	W.3.1 W.3.2 W.3.4 W.3.5 W.3.8 W.3.10
Language	L.2.4 L.2.5	L.3.4 L.3.5

Teacher Notes Pages and Reproducibles

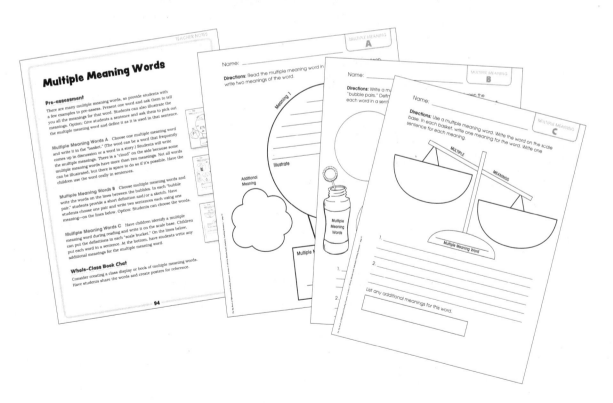

Traits

Pre-assessment

(a) Have students create a list of the character traits they know. (b) Then have students choose a character from a book they've read, or choose a character for them. Using that character, have students identify specific character traits, providing text-based evidence as support.

Traits A Choose a character, fill in the Word Box with character traits, and provide story evidence (things the character said, things the character thought, and two of the character's actions). Students will match specific traits from the Word Box to the story evidence. Option: You can leave other parts blank for students to complete based on ability.

Traits B Choose a character and fill in the character traits and/or the evidence. In the circles, students will identify if the character trait is positive (+) or negative (-). This will encourage interesting conversation when a trait appears to be both good and bad. Option: You can leave the handout blank, allowing the students to fill it in entirely.

Traits C Students will identify a character and that character's traits with supporting evidence. Then they will write an important story event involving the character. Finally, students will think about the impact of the character's traits on the characters, actions, and story events.

Whole-Class Book Chat

Have students discuss their characters' traits. What behaviors were associated with the traits? Why were the characters' traits important in the stories?

Name: _____

Directions: Using examples from the story, write specific traits of the given character. Use the Word Box or supply your own traits.

Title: _____

Character: _____

Word Box

_____   _____   _____   _____

_____   _____   _____   _____

said

thought

action taken

action taken

_____

Name: _____

Directions: Choose a character. Identify three character traits. Provide specific text-based evidence to support your choices. In each circle, decide if you think the trait is a positive trait (+) or a negative trait (−) .

- thinks
- says
- feels
- does
- travels

Title: _____

_____

Character: _____

Traits	Put the evidence in your own words.
_____ ◯	_____ _____ _____ _____
_____ ◯	_____ _____ _____ _____
_____ ◯	_____ _____ _____

Name: _____

Title: _____

1. Choose a main character. _____

2. Identify two character traits. Provide text-based evidence to support your choices.

Trait 1	Trait 2

Evidence: _____

_____

_____

_____

Evidence: _____

_____

_____

_____

3. Think about how the character's traits above impacted the character's actions in the story. Describe one important story event involving the character.

Story Event:

_____

_____

_____

_____

4. How did the character's traits impact the character's actions?

_____

_____

_____

_____

Prediction

Pre-assessment

Predictions can be made prior to or during reading. *Prior to reading:* Show students the book cover and read the title. Tell them to make a prediction and to explain why they made that prediction. *During reading:* Stop midway into the story. Have students make a prediction and provide support using story clues and details.

Prediction A   Decide if this is a before-reading or during-reading prediction. Have students check off three clues/details to help them predict, or choose the clues for them prior to reproducing. Label each clue box. Students will draw and/or write their predictions in the boxes. Then they will discuss their predictions.

Prediction B   Have students check the box and choose either a before-reading or during-reading prediction. They will draw and/or write a prediction and then choose specific evidence to support their claim. After reading, ask students to reflect. Was their prediction correct? If not, was it well-supported? If yes, have them discuss their evidence. When students reflect, they may see a prediction can be well-supported but not correct.

Prediction C   Students will gather story details to make a prediction. Students can use the handout for two predictions during their reading. After predicting, encourage students to write an "I wonder…" statement about the story. Option 1: You can provide story clues/details as a guide. Option 2: Have students explain why they made their predictions.

Whole-Class Book Chat

Have the children talk about different clues/details they used to make predictions. Discuss the use of prior knowledge and personal experiences. Discuss a before-reading prediction and a during-reading prediction. What is the difference?

Name: _____

Directions: Choose three clues or details from the Clue Box to help you make a prediction and label each box below. Draw or write information in each box to help you make a prediction.

Title: _____

```
┌─ CLUE BOX ─────────┐
│ Check three clues/details to │
│ help you predict.            │
│    ❏ title                   │
│    ❏ cover illustration      │
│    ❏ prior knowledge         │
│    ❏ illustration in story   │
│    ❏ character actions       │
│    ❏ other                   │
└──────────────────────┘
```

Clue/Detail:

Clue/Detail:

Clue/Detail:

Prediction: _____

_____

_____

_____

Name: _____

Directions: Gather information from the story, the title, the illustrations, and your own experiences. Make a prediction. Explain your thinking and provide evidence to support your prediction.

Title: _____

Check one: ❑ before reading   ❑ during reading

PREDICTION

EVIDENCE

Reflect. Was your prediction correct? If not, was it well-supported?

Name: _____

Directions: Gather story clues/details to make a prediction. Write the clues/details in the first box. Next use the story clues/details and your related knowledge to make a prediction. Then write an "I wonder…" statement as you prepare to read on. Repeat again later in the story.

Title: _____

Story Clues/Details	Story Clues/Details

So I predict…

So I predict…

? I wonder… _____
_____
_____
_____

? I wonder… _____
_____
_____
_____

Characterization

Pre-assessment

Read a story, choose a character, and have the children: (a) Describe the character (looks, emotions, interests); (b) Describe any challenges the character faced and how the character handled them; (c) Describe important actions taken by the character.

Characterization A   Choose the character. Students will write key words to fill in the boxes, following the headings. Have students use their key words to write a sentence about the character. Option 1: Students can choose the character. Option 2: The boxes can be partially filled in, depending on student need. (Discuss "interactions" as the term may be new to students.)

Characterization B   Have students focus on one specific part of the character—how he or she faces challenges and events. Students can identify the character. Then have them identify two major events and note the character's response. You can complete any section, dependent on student ability to create a modified activity for the children.

Characterization C   Have students choose a character and a story event. Then have them note how the character reacts to the specific event. Have students write how the character's actions impact the rest of the story. Children can then plan and develop a paragraph describing the character.

Whole-Class Book Chat

Children can compare characters from the books they've read and see if they can find any patterns regarding actions or behaviors. How do the characters handle challenges? How do the actions of various characters impact the stories?

Name: _____

Directions: Identify a character. In the boxes, draw and write facts about the character. Use specific details from the story. Write a sentence describing the character.

Title: _____

Looks Like	Says and Thinks	Interests

Actions		Other Character Interactions

Character: _____

Sentence: _____

Name: _____

Directions: Choose a character. Identify specific events or challenges involving that character. Write how the character responds to the specific event or challenge.

Title: _____

Character

Major Events and Challenges	Character Response

Name: _____

Directions: Choose a character. Identify one story event and the character's reaction to it. Write how the character's reaction impacts the rest of the story.

Title: _____

Character: _____

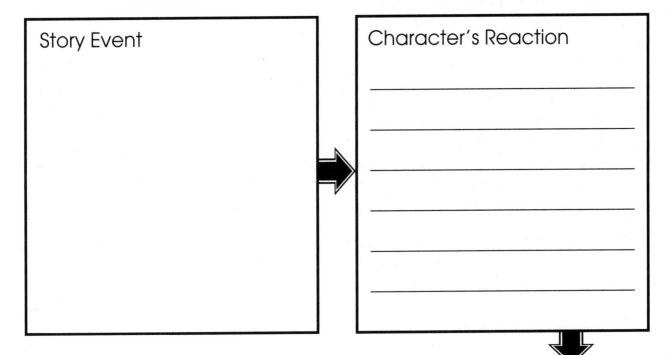

Story Event	Character's Reaction

How do the character's actions impact the rest of the story?

On a separate sheet of paper, describe the character in detail.

Think about…

- character traits
- words spoken
- motivations
- character actions
- thoughts
- feelings
- story events

Character Actions

Pre-assessment

Read a story and select a character. Have students identify three major character actions from the story. Then have them use the actions to draw a conclusion about the character.

Character Actions A   Choose a character. Have students list three things the character did in the story. Have them illustrate one of the actions and write a sentence about the character. Encourage them to include details in the drawing as well as the sentence. Option: The students will choose the character.

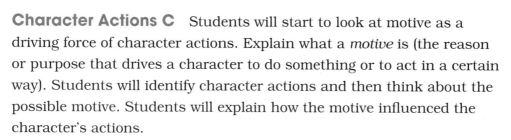

Character Actions B   Have students select a character. Then have them note one important character action. Have students think beyond the action to determine the consequence of the action and how it impacts other characters in the story. Using all the information, have students draw a conclusion about the character.

Character Actions C   Students will start to look at motive as a driving force of character actions. Explain what a *motive* is (the reason or purpose that drives a character to do something or to act in a certain way). Students will identify character actions and then think about the possible motive. Students will explain how the motive influenced the character's actions.

Whole-Class Book Chat

Have students talk about the different characters in the books they've read. Discuss some of the actions, interactions, and motives of characters and the impact those have on character actions, interactions, and personalities.

Name: _____

Directions: Focus on one character. List three things the character did in the story. Illustrate one character action from your list. Write one telling sentence about the character.

Title: _____

Include details in your illustration.

Character:

1.

2.

3.

Sentence: _____

Name: _____

Directions: Choose a character. Identify one important action taken by that character. Fill in the small boxes to show the consequence of the action and how it impacts the story.

Title: _____

Character

Character ACTION

Consequence of Action

Other Characters Impacted by This Action

Based on the character's actions, draw a conclusion about the character.

_____

_____

_____

_____

Name: _____

Directions: Identify two important actions taken by one character. Then think about why the character took those actions. What was the MOTIVE?

Title: _____

Character: _____

CHARACTER ACTIONS	MOTIVE
	What did the character want?

Describe how the character's motives influenced his or her actions.

_____

_____

_____

_____

_____

Character Change

Pre-assessment

Read a story to the class in which the character changes over the course of the story. Ask students: How did the character change from the beginning to the end? Then have students explain if this change was a good change or not a good one.

Character Change A   Choose the character. Fill in the word box with character traits and character descriptors that children can use to describe the character at either the beginning or end of the story. Students will choose three of these descriptors to write on the lines for both the beginning and the end. Then they will illustrate the character at both points in the story.

Character Change B   Students can choose a character. In the boxes, students can take notes, using key words to describe the character at the beginning and at the end of the story. Using these key words, have students write an explanation of the character's change.

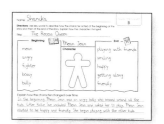

Character Change C   Students are again noting character change, but they are also exploring why the change took place. Then students will evaluate if the change had a positive or negative impact. When students finish, have them discuss their observations by using story details to explain what the character learned and either gained or lost by changing.

Whole-Class Book Chat

Students can discuss how their characters changed over time. Different characters may respond to different events. By charting them, children can start to see patterns in character behaviors. Students can also discuss positive and negative changes and begin to understand character development.

Name: _____

Directions: Note how the character changed over time. Use the Word Box words to help you.

Title: _____

Character: _____

_____   _____   _____   _____

_____   _____   _____   _____

Beginning

List three words.

_____

_____

_____

Illustrate in the box.

End

List three words.

_____

_____

_____

Illustrate in the box.

Name: _____

Directions: Use key words to describe how the character acted at the beginning of the story and then at the end of the story. Explain how the character changed.

Title: _____

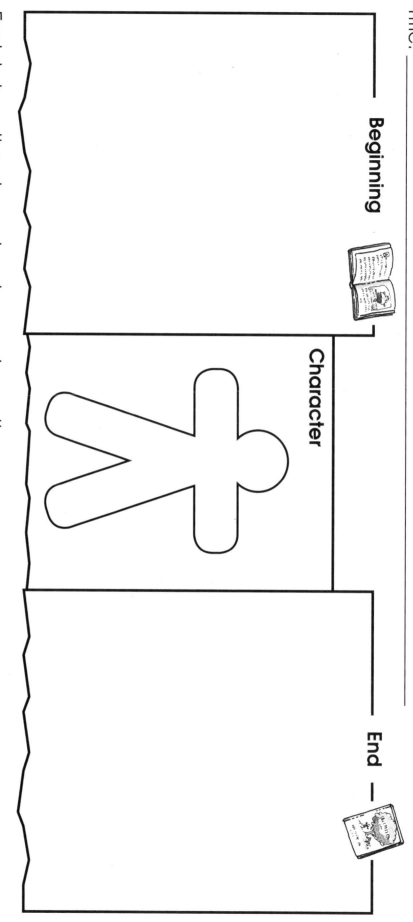

Beginning

Character

End

Explain how the character changed over time.

_____
_____
_____

Name: _____

Directions: Think about how the character changed over time throughout the story.

Title: _____

WHO?	
HOW did the character change?	WHY did the character change?

Color.

 positive change

 negative change

Main Idea

Please Note: These reproducibles can be used with fiction or nonfiction.

Pre-assessment

Read a fiction or nonfiction story or excerpt to children and have them identify the main idea of the selection. Ask them to include one to three details that help support the main idea.

Main Idea A   This handout will need to be copied single-sided because students will be cutting it out. Write the main idea on it before copying. Then students can fill in the "leaves" with the title and two supporting details. Students will cut out the leaves and paste them on the stem. Option: Fill in the details and have students identify the main idea.

Main Idea B   Students will complete the title or headline. You will identify the topic. Then students can write the main idea and details. Option 1: You can have students identify the topic. Option 2: You can fill in part of the handout if the need is evident.

Main Idea C   Students will identify the main idea and supporting details. Students should include key words, the precursor to note-taking and outlining. The children will identify the author's reason for writing this piece.

Whole-Class Book Chat

Children can discuss the main ideas presented in various stories and texts. Some may overlap which can lead to an interesting discussion. Students can also discuss how they determined the main idea and how the details are used to support the author's focus.

Name: _____

Directions: Write the main idea in the flower. Write the title and details in the leaves. Cut out the leaves and paste them on the stem.

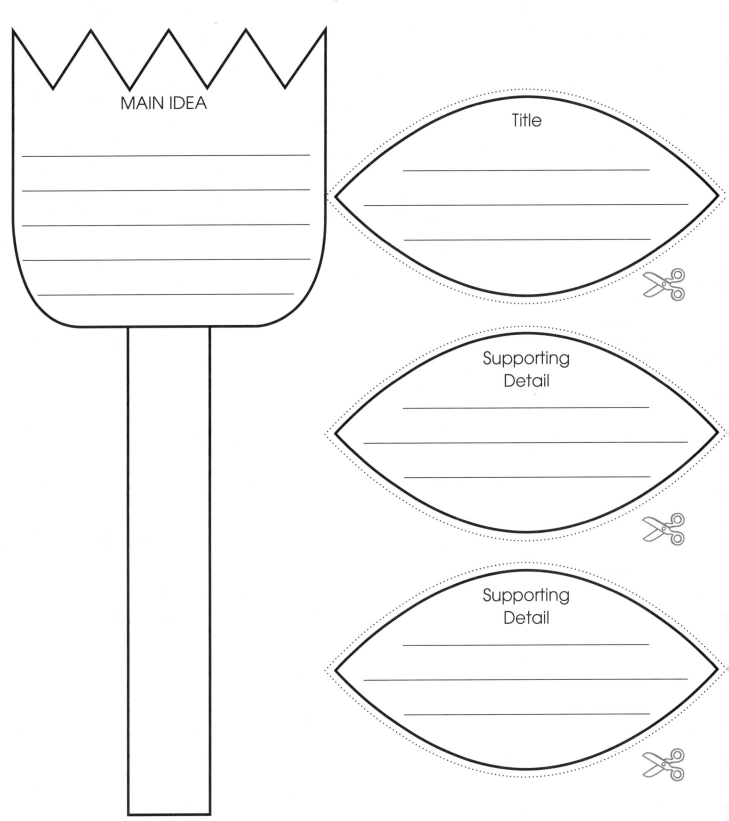

MAIN IDEA

Title

Supporting Detail

Supporting Detail

Name: _____

Directions: Identify the topic, main idea, and supporting details.

Title/Headline: _____

_____

Topic:

Main Idea: _____

_____

_____

_____

_____

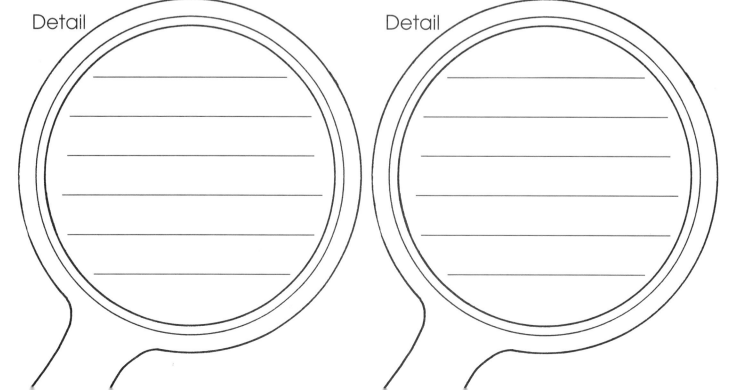

Detail

Detail

The Big Book of Differentiated Reading Response Activities © 2014 by Rhonda Graff, Scholastic Teaching Resources • page 36

Name: _____

Directions: Identify the main idea and supporting details. List any key words. Answer the question below.

Title/Headline: _____

_____

Main Idea _____

_____

_____

_____

_____

Supporting Details

Key Words

_____

_____

_____

_____

Key Words

Why did the author write this?

_____

_____

_____

_____

Simile

Pre-assessment

Stories and poetry can be used to share similes with young children. Read a simile first within the context of a story or a poem and then read another isolated simile. For each simile ask: What does the simile mean? What is being compared?

Simile A   Write the simile in the box prior to reproducing. Students will illustrate the two things being compared. You can fill in the lines identifying what is being compared. Students need to fill in the oval telling what is common to both. Options: Students can fill in the comparison lines on the chart. This page can be used with any simile. It does not have to come from a story or article.

Simile B   Write the simile in the box. Students will identify what is being compared and what trait the two items have in common. They will also need to think about how the simile helps them create better pictures in their minds and aids their understanding. Option: Students can either write a given simile or find one on their own.

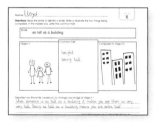

Simile C   This level includes similar response opportunities as above, but it extends the children's thinking by having them reflect about why a writer would choose to use a given simile.

Whole-Class Book Chat

Children can share the similes they encounter and discuss why they are used. Consider making a class book so the children can revisit the similes and add to them as the year progresses. Understanding the use of simile can help improve the students' writing skills as well.

Name: _____

Directions: Read the simile. Illustrate what is being compared. Fill in the blanks below to support your drawing. In the oval, write what is common to both words being compared.

Simile:

Illustrate.   Illustrate.

_____ is compared to _____

What is common to both?

_____

_____

_____

Name: _____

SIMILE

B

Directions: Read the simile or identify a simile. Write or illustrate the two things being compared. In the middle box, write the common trait.

Simile: _____

| Object 1 | Common Trait | Compared to Object 2 |

Describe how the simile causes you to change your image of Object 1.

_____

_____

Name: _____

Directions: Identify a simile. Illustrate the simile as it is used in the story. Write your responses to the questions below.

Title: _____

Simile

Illustrate the simile.

What is the author trying to say? How does the use of simile in this story help you understand the author's vision?

_____

_____

_____

_____

_____

_____

Retell

Note About Retell: Retelling, a valuable comprehension skill, is different from summarizing. Retelling is usually done orally, but some teachers have students write their retellings since we can't always meet with each student. Use these reproducibles as supports to help students remember key events. Including the author's message is a higher level skill, one that requires a deeper understanding of the story. It is included in Retell B and C only as scaffolding for summarizing.

Pre-assessment

Choose an appropriate level story to read aloud. Distribute paper so children can sketch or take notes. After reading, have the children retell the story. Children can use pictures, key words, or sentences. (Verbal responses can be shared.)

Retell A   Students are encouraged to use pictures and key words to help them remember the important parts of the story. Have children verbally share the story. Fill in any part(s) as needed to help children focus on key points of the story.

Retell B   Some of the supports have been removed, and students are responsible for filling in the key parts with key words. In addition, students are asked to note the author's message.

Retell C   Students will think of story structure. They will note how the story begins, how the story action starts, and then how it rises to a climax and subsides. The students might also be aware of the author's message. Students will use key words to help support their retelling.

Whole-Class Book Chat

Students can use the class chat as a way to share and recommend literature to their peers. Students can be creative with their retellings and perform a puppet play, a skit, or do a Readers' Theater.

Name: _____

Directions: Use pictures and words to help you retell the story.

1. *Introduction*	Title: Author:	
2. *Beginning*		
3. *Middle*	Then	PROBLEM
	Next	
	After	
4. *End*	SOLUTION?	

Name: _____

Directions: Make notes to help you retell the story aloud. Use key words, important phrases, and pictures. Decide the author's message.

Title: _____

Beginning
- **Characters**
- **Setting**

Middle
- **Story events**

Conclusion

AUTHOR'S MESSAGE

Name: _____

Directions: Use key words to walk down "Story Lane." Retell the story aloud. Answer the question below.

Title: _____

4. _____

_____

_____

_____

3. _____   5. _____

_____   _____

_____   _____

_____   _____

2. _____   _____

_____   6. _____

_____   _____

_____   _____

1. _____   _____

_____   _____

_____   _____

_____   _____

STORY LANE

What is the author's message? _____

_____

_____

_____

Conflict

Pre-assessment

Share a story with students and have them identify the story problem, the solution (if there is one), and the characters involved. If there is more than one problem, they can identify that as well.

Conflict A Fill in any of the boxes before copying, providing support where needed. Have students identify the problem and the characters involved. Then they can address how the problem is solved. If there are other conflicts, they can write these as well. In the boxes, _____ vs. _____, students can identify the main conflict. (Discuss "vs." although many children will be familiar with it from video games.)

Conflict B Students will identify the problem including specific details from the story. Then they will identify if the problem is solved and how, also using text evidence. Finally, students will tell what the characters learn, which is often the story's lesson.

Conflict C Students identify the conflict. At this level, students may be better able to understand conflict in terms such as "man vs. man," but some children may need to be more specific. Students will identify when the problem started and if the problem was solved. Then students will provide an alternative solution.

Whole-Class Book Chat

Students can discuss the different conflicts found in their books. By keeping track of the different types of conflicts students can learn about story structure. Class discussions can focus on the importance of conflict in story development. Students might also be exposed to various types of conflicts beyond character vs. character.

Name: _____

Directions: Answer the questions below. Write key words or sentences. Draw pictures and add labels.

Title: _____

What is the problem?	Who are the characters involved?

| CONFLICT |
| VS. |

How was the problem solved?	Identify any other conflicts in the story.

Name: _____

Directions: Identify the conflict. Think about what the author wanted to say through this story conflict.

Title: _____

DR. PROBLEM	What is the problem? Use specific details from the story.	CAPTAIN SOLUTION	How is the problem solved? Use specific details from the story.
_____ _____ _____ _____ _____ _____ _____ _____		_____ _____ _____ _____ _____ _____ _____ _____	

What did the characters learn?

_____
_____
_____
_____
_____
_____
_____
_____

Name: _____

Directions: Use the headings below to help learn more about the story conflict.

Title: _____

VS. _____

What is one conflict? (There may be more than one.)

_____

_____

Was the problem resolved?   Yes   No   Explain.

_____

_____

_____

_____

_____

_____

_____

_____

Explain how the problem began. Who was involved?

_____

_____

_____

_____

_____

_____

_____

_____

On the back of this sheet, write another way this problem could have been solved.

Fact and Opinion

Please Note: These reproducibles can be used with fiction or nonfiction.

Pre-assessment

(a) Present students with various statements and have them verbally identify whether each one is a fact or an opinion. (b) Then share a story (use either fiction or nonfiction) and have students list two facts from the text and two opinions. This is a bit more challenging as they need to understand the story or text.

Fact and Opinion A   Prepare the handout prior to copying. In the dotted boxes at the bottom, fill in two correct facts related to the topic and two incorrect facts or general opinions. Students will choose two correct facts from the choices presented and paste them in the "dish." Then they will write three opinions of their own in the ice cream scoops.

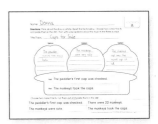

Fact and Opinion B   Students are asked to provide their own facts and an opinion. Next to the ruler, a factual tool, students record topic-related facts. Next to the paintbrush, students express their own opinions. Students will support their viewpoints, explaining what led them to their opinions.

Fact and Opinion C   Prepare this activity prior to reproducing. In Box A, write an opinion. Students will read it, decide if they agree with it, and check the appropriate box on the ticket. Then students will defend their response using facts from the story. Option: Have students write an opinion in Box A and defend it. They will not need to check the ticket.

Whole-Class Book Chat

Students can discuss what they are reading (fiction and nonfiction) and create fact and opinion charts. This will encourage lively discussions, as children will not always agree with one another.

Name: _____

Directions: Think about the story or article. Read the facts below. Choose two correct facts and paste them in the dish. Then write your opinions about the topic in the three scoops.

Title/Topic: _____

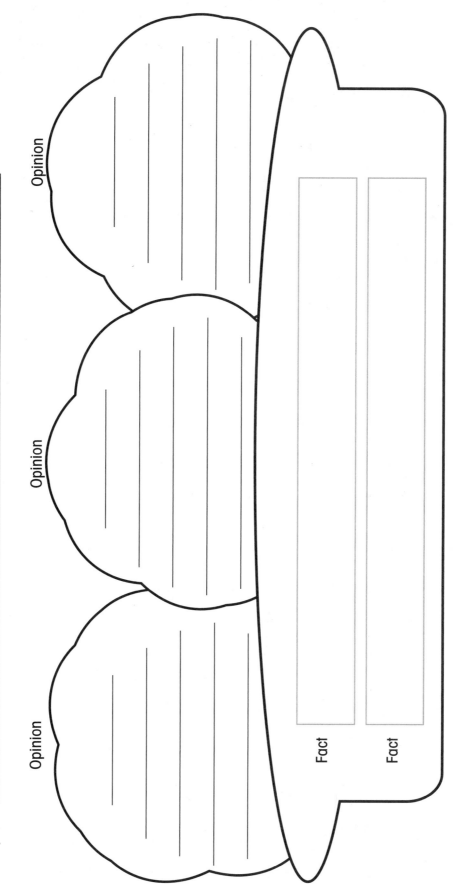

Opinion

Opinion

Opinion

Fact

Fact

Choose two correct facts. Cut them out and paste them in the dish.

Name: _____

Directions: Choose a topic if one is not provided. Next to the ruler write facts about the topic. Then next to the paintbrush write your opinion about the same subject. Support your opinion and tell why you feel that way.

Topic: _____

The facts measure up!

_____

_____

_____

_____

_____

Paint an opinion. Support your opinion. Tell why.

Opinion _____

_____

_____

_____

Support _____

_____

_____

_____

_____

Name: _____

Directions: Read the opinion in Box A. Decide if you agree or disagree and check the correct box. Defend your response with factual information. If you write your own opinion, leave the ticket blank.

Box A

❏ agree
❏ disagree

Defend your opinion. Use facts to support your opinion.

Compare and Contrast

Pre-assessment

(a) Choose two topics familiar to the children. Ask them to compare and contrast the topics. (b) Then read a story and choose two characters for the children to compare and contrast. Some students may draw and some may write.

Compare and Contrast A   Prior to reproducing, write two items or people being compared/contrasted on the lines provided. Using the visuals in the text, have students write similarities in the apples and write a sentence highlighting the similarities. Then have them write the differences in the pear and the orange and write a sentence highlighting the differences.

Compare and Contrast B   Provide a focus story element (setting, characters, conflict, or solution) prior to reproducing. Students will write the titles of two different books in the boxes. Then they will compare and contrast them using the Venn diagram. Students need to draw a conclusion about the books.

Compare and Contrast C   Students will be comparing/contrasting two characters from the same book who interact in some way. Identify the attributes and write them in the chart prior to reproducing. Some attributes include: kindness, honesty, respect, responsibility, self-control, trustworthiness, or perseverance. Then students will complete the chart and draw a conclusion about BOTH characters.

Whole-Class Book Chat

Since there will be a variety of books being read, children can discuss the similarities and differences among the books. They can focus on specific characters, themes, settings, or authors. Certain patterns may emerge.

Name: _____

Directions: Compare and contrast. In the apples, use key words to note the similarities. In the pear and orange, use key words to note the differences. Then write one sentence for the similarities and one sentence for the differences.

COMPARE AND CONTRAST

_____ and _____

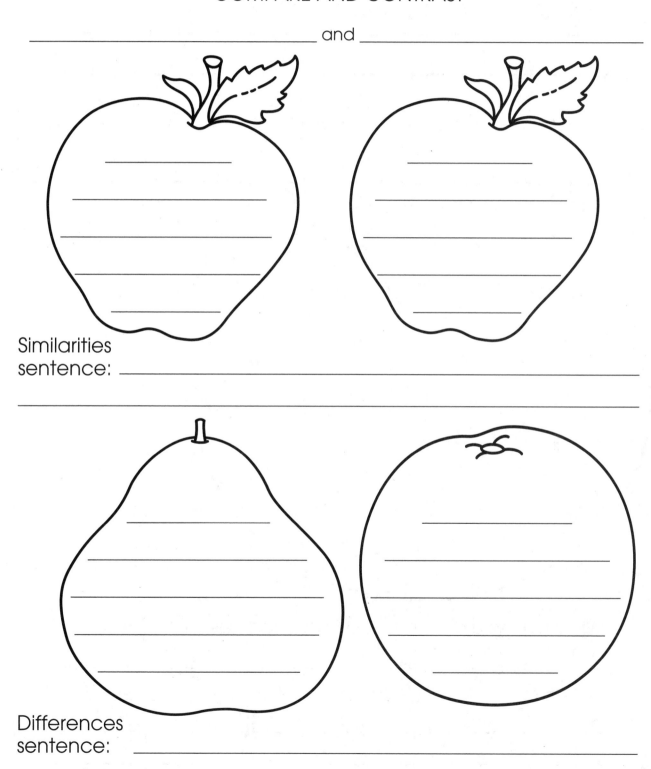

Similarities
sentence: _____

_____

Differences
sentence: _____

_____

Name: _____

Directions: Focus on the story element provided. Compare and contrast using two different texts.

Focus:

Title of Book 1:

Title of Book 2:

What can you conclude from the Venn diagram?

_____

_____

_____

_____

Name: _____

Directions: Choose two characters from the same book. Use the chart below to focus on their attributes. Draw a conclusion based on their similarities and differences.

Title: _____

Attributes	Character 1	Character 2
	1.	2.
Attribute 1 ____		
Attribute 2 ____		

Draw a conclusion about the two characters above. How are they alike or different?

_____

_____

_____

Idiom

Pre-assessment

Present children with two idioms. They can be presented orally or written. Have students draw the literal meaning and then ask them to identify the actual meaning. Ask them to use the idiom appropriately in a sentence.

Idiom A   Prior to reproducing, write an idiom in the box. First, have students draw the literal meaning in the left box. Then have a discussion with the students about the actual meaning of the idiom. As a group, have students fill in the box at the bottom that says, "It really means." Then students can illustrate the actual meaning of the idiom in the box on the right. Be sure to model this so students understand the difference between *literal* and *actual*.

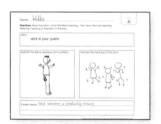

Idiom B   Choose an idiom and write it prior to reproducing. After defining the idiom, students will illustrate the literal and actual meanings. Then students will demonstrate understanding by using the idiom in two sentences. Option: The students can choose an idiom.

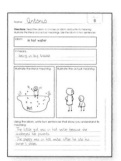

Idiom C   Supply the idiom. Students will write its meaning. Students will need to think about when a writer would use this idiom and the message conveyed by the idiom. Students will write a sentence using the idiom. Option: Students can choose their own idiom and complete the page.

Whole-Class Book Chat

Children can share the idioms they hear day to day. The class can keep an ongoing list for reference and students can act out skits using the idioms. Children can also note the use of idioms in stories or poems, discussing the reason a writer might choose to use one.

Name: _____

Directions: Read the idiom. Draw the literal meaning. Then draw the true meaning. Write the meaning of the idiom in the box.

Idiom:

Illustrate the literal meaning (as it is written).

Illustrate the meaning of the idiom.

It really means _____
_____

Name: _____

Directions: Read the idiom or choose an idiom and write its meaning.
Illustrate the literal and actual meanings. Use the idiom in two sentences.

Idiom:

It means...

_____

_____

Illustrate the literal meaning.	Illustrate the actual meaning.

Using the idiom, write two sentences that show you understand its
meaning.

_____

_____

_____

_____

Name: _____

Directions: Read the idiom or choose an idiom. Define it. Think about how it's used and answer the questions. Use the idiom in a sentence.

Idiom: _____

means: _____
_____

_____

WRITER'S
TOOLBOX

When might a writer choose to use this idiom?

_____
_____
_____

What message would a writer want to share by using this idiom?

_____
_____
_____

Use the idiom in a sentence.

_____
_____
_____

Setting

Pre-assessment

Ask students: What is the setting of a story? Read the class a story and have students identify the setting at the beginning of it. Have them note if the setting changes throughout the story. Children can also illustrate the setting. Encourage them to provide a caption or label their illustrations.

Setting A   Students will identify the setting at the *beginning* of the story by using key words. They can also provide information through an illustration in the box provided. As the story progresses, have students note if there is a change in the setting. If so, have them complete the key word list and illustrate the *new setting*.

Setting B   Students will focus on the importance of the setting to that particular story. In the first column, have them write key words or draw a picture to describe the setting. In the second column, have them identify the importance of that setting to the story.

Setting C   Students will describe the setting and think about the author's decision to choose that setting for the story. They will write how the setting affects the mood. Students can discuss what impact a change in setting would have on the story.

Whole-Class Book Chat

Students can use their personal book settings to help create a settings list. Then discuss the impact these settings have on the stories and the characters. Describe any changes in setting in any of the books. What moods were created?

Name: _____

Directions: Identify the BEGINNING SETTING. List any key words that describe the setting. Then illustrate the setting. As the story progresses if the setting changes, complete the NEW SETTING portion the same way.

Title: _____

BEGINNING SETTING	NEW SETTING
List key words:	List key words:

BEGINNING SETTING

List key words:

_____

_____

_____

_____

_____

_____

Illustrate the setting at the beginning of the story.

NEW SETTING

List key words:

_____

_____

_____

_____

_____

_____

Illustrate another setting at a different point in the story.

Name: _____

Directions: Describe the setting. Why is the setting important to the story?

Title: _____

Setting • Illustrate • Use key words and phrases	Why is the setting important to the story?

Name: _____

Directions: Shed some light on the setting. Identify the setting in the light beam. Note if it changes. Then answer the setting-related questions.

Title: _____

Using key words, describe the setting. Note setting changes.

_____

_____

_____

_____

_____

How does the setting affect the mood of the story?

_____

_____

_____

_____

_____

_____

_____

_____

_____

_____

_____

Why did the author choose this setting?

_____

_____

_____

_____

_____

_____

_____

_____

Questioning

Please Note: These reproducibles can be used with fiction or nonfiction.

Pre-assessment

Present a topic of common interest (school, friends, sports, music) to the class and have students write two questions about the topic. Option 1: Read a book and have students compose questions about the story. Option 2: Allow students to create an illustration of their choice. Students can give their drawings to a partner and have the partner write two questions about it.

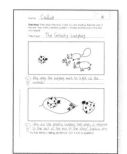

Questioning A   Students will respond to a text they are reading by creating an illustration and composing a question about the illustration/text. They can repeat the process at another point in the text. To extend students' thinking, have them write a statement about the text and then turn it into a question.

Questioning B   Have students use the question leads (*who, what, when,* and *why*) to begin sentences about the text. Then they make a prediction by answering one of their questions.

Questioning C   Students will identify an event and write why the event is important. Then the children will expand their thinking and ask a question related to the event. Have them repeat this process for another event.

Whole-Class Book Chat

Students can chat about the use of questions and how they help readers better understand and think about what they read. Children can pose questions about one another's texts.

Name: _____

Directions: Think about the story or text you are reading. Illustrate part of the text. Then write a related question. Choose another part of the text and repeat.

Title/Topic: _____

? _____
_____

? _____
_____

Try this! Write a telling sentence. Turn it into a question.

Name: _____

Directions: Using your knowledge of the story or article, pose questions for each question word. Make a prediction. In the blank rainbow arches, make up your own questions.

Title: _____

WHO

WHAT

WHEN

WHY

Choose one of your questions and answer it in a complete sentence below.

_____

_____

Name: _____

Directions: Identify an event. Tell why it is important. Then "expand your thinking" and write a question about the event.

Title: _____

Event 1

_____

_____

_____

_____

E-X-P-A-N-D your thinking.

Why is this event important?

_____

_____

_____

Event 2

_____

_____

_____

_____

E-X-P-A-N-D your thinking.

Why is this event important?

_____

_____

_____

Point of View and Perspective

Pre-assessment

(a) To identify point of view, read a story or story part and ask the children to identify who is telling the story. (b) To see if children can understand character perspective, read another story (or excerpt) where characters see a particular event differently. Ask children how each of the characters view the event.

Point of View and Perspective A   Students are asked to write a book title and identify who is telling the story. Although first-person, second-person, and third-person point of view is not introduced formally, students can say a specific character is telling the story, or a narrator is telling the story. In the speech bubble, have students write who is telling the story. Then have students decide whether the person telling the story is actually in the story or not. A character will be in the story, but a narrator will not. There is room on the handout for students to do this activity with two different books.

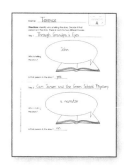

Point of View and Perspective B   Choose a story event in which two characters see the same event differently. Provide the characters and the event. Students will write the characters' perspectives and feelings about the event. Option: Students will identify the events and the characters themselves.

Point of View and Perspective C   Students will identify who is telling the story. They will choose a specific event in the story. Students will choose a different character, other than the actual narrator, and note how that character would provide a different perspective of the same event.

Whole-Class Book Chat

Collect various books. Have students read and share parts of the stories, allowing them to determine who is telling each story. Option: Students can expressively read aloud a section of text, demonstrating two characters' perspectives about a common event. Children can discuss how that would impact the story.

Name: _____

Directions: Identify who is telling the story. Decide if that person is in the story. There is room for two different books.

Title 1: _____

Who is telling
the story?

Is that person in the story? _____

Title 2: _____

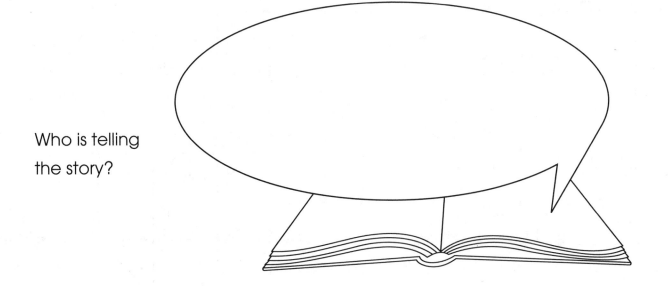

Who is telling
the story?

Is that person in the story? _____

Name: _____

Directions: Using a specific story event, note how two characters see the same event.
Write each character's perspective.

Title: _____

Character:	Story Event	Character:

Name: _____

Directions: Identify the point of view. Who is telling the story?
Answer the questions below.

Title: _____

Who is telling the story?

_____

_____

_____

Narrator?

Character?

Someone else?

Choose a specific event in the story.

_____

_____

_____

Choose a different character as narrator.

_____

How would that narrator provide a different perspective?
Explain how the story would differ.

_____

_____

_____

_____

_____

_____

_____

_____

Theme

Note on Theme: Theme is a challenging concept for many young readers. Fill in the theme as needed and encourage discussion so students can begin to understand, and become familiar with, various themes in literature. Modeling is very important.

Pre-assessment

Read a story to students and ask them to identify the story theme or story message. Ask them to explain what happened in the story to support their claims. Note: Fables and fairy tales offer clear messages while some other stories can be more challenging.

Theme A Prior to reproducing, provide the theme on the Story Message line. Take time to discuss the theme before students write anything. Students will then write the meaning of the theme in their own words. They will identify one character who would benefit from the message or lesson and use story details to tell why.

Theme B Fill in the story details prior to reproducing. This will allow students to work from part to whole to identify the theme. Option: The teacher can fill in the theme and have students work from whole to part as they find details to support the theme. Once the theme and details are determined, students can decide how the theme relates to the characters.

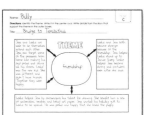

Theme C In the large oval, students will write the theme. In the rectangles, they will write supporting details from the text.

Whole-Class Book Chat

Students can discuss the various themes they come across in their readings. Even though the themes may be the same, they will see that the supporting details may differ.

Name: _____

Directions: Read the theme or story message. Put it in your own words. Answer the question below.

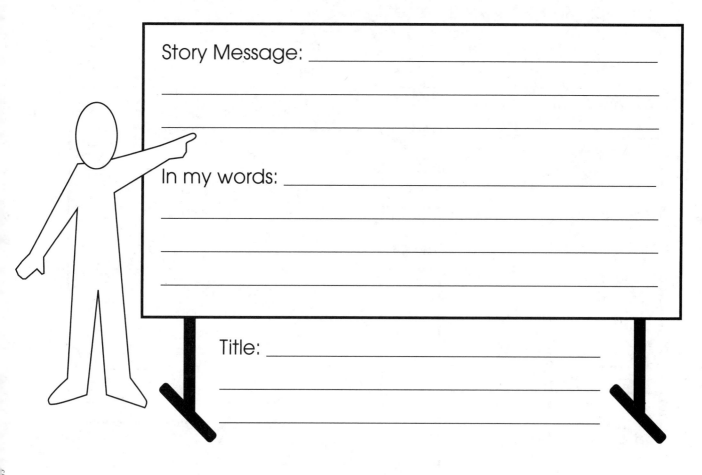

Story Message: _____

_____

_____

In my words: _____

_____

_____

_____

Title: _____

_____

_____

Which character could benefit from learning the story message? Include an example from the story to support your response.

Character: _____

Support: _____

_____

_____

_____

_____

_____

Name: _____

Directions: Determine the theme (story message) based on the story details provided. OR Determine the supporting details based on the theme provided. Answer the question below.

Title: _____

Text-based Story Details	THEME or LESSON

How does the story theme (message) relate to the characters in the story?

Name: _____

Directions: Identify the theme. Write it in the center oval. Write details from the story that support the theme in the outer boxes.

Title: _____

THEME

Summarize

> **Note on Summarizing:** Summarizing is a very challenging skill. Be sure your students are ready for this. Spend plenty of time modeling and reviewing, modeling, and modeling some more before you ask students to do this independently.
>
> Note: These reproducibles can be used with fiction or nonfiction.

Pre-assessment

Choose a fictional story or a nonfiction piece. Provide children with a handout to help guide them. It should include: *who, what, where, when, why,* and *how.* Students can write a summary using the question words as a guide.

Summarize A   Students will use illustrations and key words to identify *who, what, where, when,* and *why.* They will use the key words to share a summary orally.

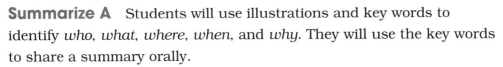

Summarize B   Students will continue to identify *who, what, where, when,* and *why* with key words and illustrations. Children at this level will write the summary by "adding up" the details. It will be challenging for students to keep this short.

Summarize C   Students continue to use the question words and key words or pictures to highlight important information. Have them write a summary. Encourage them to keep it short and focused on key points only.

Whole-Class Book Chat

Children can share their summaries and focus on identifying the most important facts and details in the stories and articles shared.

Name: _____

Directions: Use key words and pictures to summarize the story or article.

Title: _____

Who?

_____
_____
_____

When?

What?

_____
_____
_____
_____

_____
_____
_____

When?

Where?

_____
_____

Why?

_____
_____
_____
_____
_____
_____
_____

Name: _____

Directions: "Add up" the key points in the story. Draw pictures or write key words in each box. Write a summary below.

WHO?	

WHAT?	

WHERE AND WHEN?	

+

WHY?	

Title: _____

Summary: _____

_____

_____

_____

_____

Name: _____

Directions: Complete the "big picture" frames using key words and phrases. Draw or write. Write a summary below.

Title: _____

Who? or What?

When? and Where?

Problem? What happened?

Solution (Solved? How? Why?)

Summary: _____

Cause and Effect

Pre-assessment

(a) Present students with three isolated situations of cause and effect and a blank t-chart. Provide a cause and ask for an effect or provide an effect and ask for a cause. (b) Read a story to students and have them identify the cause and effect. Option: Based on the story, provide a cause, an effect, or neither, varying the degree of what is expected from students. Have them identify the missing part(s).

Cause and Effect A Supply either the cause or the effect. Option: Both can be left blank if the children are ready to find all the information.

Cause and Effect B Fill in either the cause or the effect prior to reproducing. Students will fill in what is missing on the handout. At the bottom of the handout, students can think about what might happen if the cause remains the same, and what impact that would have on the story. The answers must work within the confines of the story. Option: Students can fill in both the cause and effect.

Cause and Effect C Fill in Event 1 prior to reproducing. Have students fill in the subsequent boxes, noting the relationship of cause and effect throughout a story. Students are asked to reflect on the author's decision to include a specific event. Discuss how the story would change if the events were different. Option 1: Students can choose Event 1 independently and work from there. Option 2: Fill in Event 2 causing students to identify the cause of Event 2 and the effect of Event 2.

Whole-Class Book Chat

The goal here is for students to understand that each event impacts the next event. Have students discuss the different examples of cause and effect in their stories. As a group, students can think of scenarios and possible effects.

Name: _____

Directions: Complete the cause and effect boxes below. Use the information provided. The *cause* is the reason something happens. The *effect* is what happens.

Title: _____

CAUSE

EFFECT

The cause is _____
_____
_____

The effect is _____
_____
_____

Name: _____

Directions: Complete the cause and effect boxes. Then answer the questions below.

Title: _____

CAUSE — WHY something happens	EFFECT — WHAT happens

If the cause remains the same, what is another possible effect? How would the story change?

_____

_____

_____

_____

_____

Name: _____

Directions: Complete the story boxes by showing how each event caused the next event to occur. Then answer the question below.

Title: _____

cause → effect

EVENT 1	**EVENT 2**	**EVENT 3**

cause → effect

Circle Event 1 or Event 2. Why do you think the author included this event in the story?

_____

_____

_____

Classify and Sort

Please Note: These reproducibles can be used with fiction or nonfiction.

Pre-assessment

Present children with an assortment of words and tell them to sort and classify them. Note the categories chosen by the students. Let them label each group and verbally explain why they grouped the words that way.

Classify and Sort A   Fill in the Title/Topic, the headings, and the Word Box words prior to reproducing. Students will read the given headings and sort each word in the Word Box into a "bucket." Option: Over time, the children may be able to choose the Title/Topic and/or the headings on their own.

Classify and Sort B   Choose the title or topic and write the headings. Students will use the headings to find words in the story/article to sort and classify. Students will choose a word from each group then compose a sentence using at least two of those words.

Classify and Sort C   Choose the title or topic. Students will brainstorm words related to the topic on a scrap piece of paper. Using those words, students will create three headings and then sort the words into the three groups. Once the words are sorted, the children must explain how they determined the groups. Then students will choose a word from each group and write two related sentences. Option: Students will choose the topic.

Whole-Class Book Chat

Students can talk about the books they've read, noting various groupings. For fiction, group headings might include: strong characters and weak characters. For nonfiction, groupings will be topic specific.

Name: _____

Directions: Using the headings provided, sort the words in the Word Box. Put each word in a "bucket." Add your own related words to each "bucket."

Title/Topic: _____
_____

WORD BOX

Name: _____

Directions: Using the book or article presented, sort related words into the correct "bins." Give each group of words a heading.

Title/Topic: _____

Circle one word from each group. Write one sentence using at least two of those words.

Sentence: _____

_____

_____

Name: _____

Directions: Using the story, article, or activity, brainstorm related words on scrap paper. Sort the words into three groups below. Create three headings. Then complete the prompts below the chart.

Title/Topic: _____

Heading 1	Heading 2	Heading 3

Explain how you determined the three groups above. _____
_____
_____
_____

Choose a word from each group. Write two related sentences using those words.
_____
_____

Interesting Language

Pre-assessment

This concept is a bit more challenging to pre-assess. Provide children with strong examples of interesting language. Have them comment on the language. Ask them: What is the author saying? Why did the writer choose to say it that way?

Interesting Language A   Pre-select the section of text and write it in Box A. Make sure students understand what a quote is and the use of quotation marks. Have students interpret what is being said and what the author wants the reader to know. The children then illustrate what they visualize and write words to match. Check for accurate interpretation of quote.

Interesting Language B   Identify interesting quotes and copy them in the "Author's Words" sections. Have students circle any interesting language. Students will interpret the quote and write their understanding of it in the "It means..." sections. Option: Students can choose their own quotes from the text. Check for accurate interpretation of quotes.

Interesting Language C   Students will choose their own quotes during reading. In order for children to do this independently, you will need to model continually and extensively, and think out loud to identify well-written passages. Once the students find the quotes and write them correctly, they will interpret the author's words and state why they chose each quote. Check for accurate interpretation of quotes.

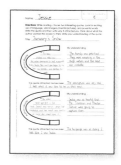

Whole-Class Book Chat

Sharing interesting quotes and fabulous words is a great way for children to start to recognize special language and to heighten their awareness. During Whole-Class Book Chats, allow children to share what they discover. Be sure to share what you come across in your reading as well.

Name: _____

Directions: Read the section of text in Box A below. Draw or write in your own words what you think the author wanted the reader to know. Underline any interesting words.

Title: _____

BOX A

I think the author is saying…

Illustrate

_____

_____

_____

_____

_____

Name: _____

Directions: Read the sections of text in the "Author's Words" boxes. Think about how the author chose certain words to convey a message or create a feeling. Circle any interesting words. In your own words, write what the author wanted to convey.

Title: _____

Author's Words	It means....

Author's Words	It means....

Name: _____

Directions: While reading, choose two interesting quotes. Look for exciting use of language, vivid imagery (mental pictures), and powerful words. Write the quote and then write why it attracted you. Think about what the author wanted the reader to think. Write your understanding of the quote.

Title: _____

Author's Quote

"
_____
_____
_____
_____

My understanding . . .

_____
_____
_____
_____
_____

This quote attracted me because _____

_____

Author's Quote

"
_____
_____
_____
_____

My understanding . . .

_____
_____
_____
_____
_____

This quote attracted me because _____

_____

Multiple Meaning Words

Pre-assessment

There are many multiple meaning words, so provide students with a few examples to pre-assess. Present one word and ask them to tell you all the meanings for that word. Students can also illustrate the meanings. Option: Give students a sentence and ask them to pick out the multiple meaning word and define it as it is used in that sentence.

Multiple Meaning Words A

Choose one multiple meaning word and write it in the "basket." (The word can be a word that frequently comes up in discussion or a word in a story.) Students will write the multiple meanings. There is a "cloud" on the side because some multiple meaning words have more than two meanings. Not all words can be illustrated, but there is space to do so if it's possible. Have the children use the word orally in sentences.

Multiple Meaning Words B

Choose multiple meaning words and write the words on the lines between the bubbles. In each "bubble pair," students provide a short definition and/or a sketch. Have students choose one pair and write two sentences each using one meaning—on the lines below. Option: Students can choose the words.

Multiple Meaning Words C

Have children identify a multiple meaning word during reading and write it on the scale base. Children can put the definitions in each "scale bucket." On the lines below, put each word in a sentence. At the bottom, have students write any additional meanings for the multiple meaning word.

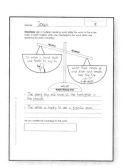

Whole-Class Book Chat

Consider creating a class display or book of multiple meaning words. Have students share the words and create posters for reference.

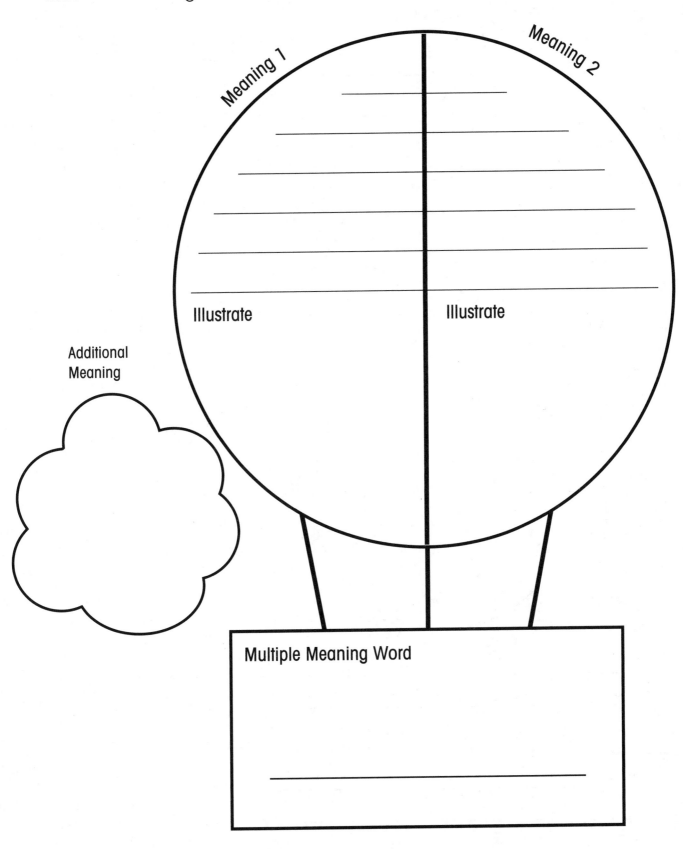

Name: _____

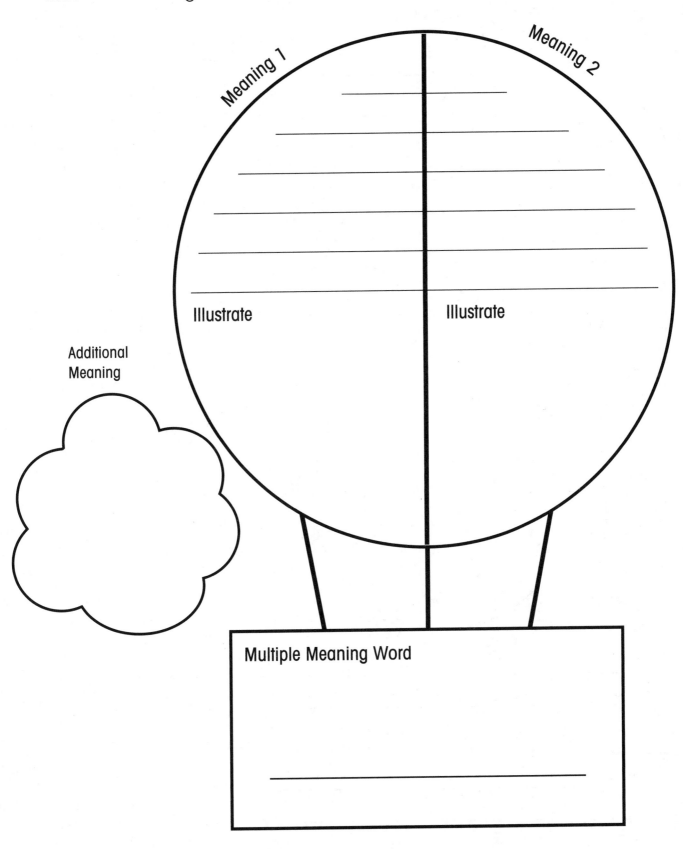

Directions: Read the multiple meaning word in the bucket. In the balloon, write two meanings of the word.

Meaning 1

Meaning 2

Illustrate

Illustrate

Additional
Meaning

Multiple Meaning Word

Name: _____

Directions: Write a multiple meaning word on the line between the "bubble pairs." Define and/or illustrate each word. Pick one pair and put each word in a sentence below.

Multiple Meaning Words

1. _____

_____

_____

2. _____

_____

_____

Name: _____

Directions: Use a multiple meaning word. Write the word on the scale base. In each basket, write one meaning for the word. Write one sentence for each meaning.

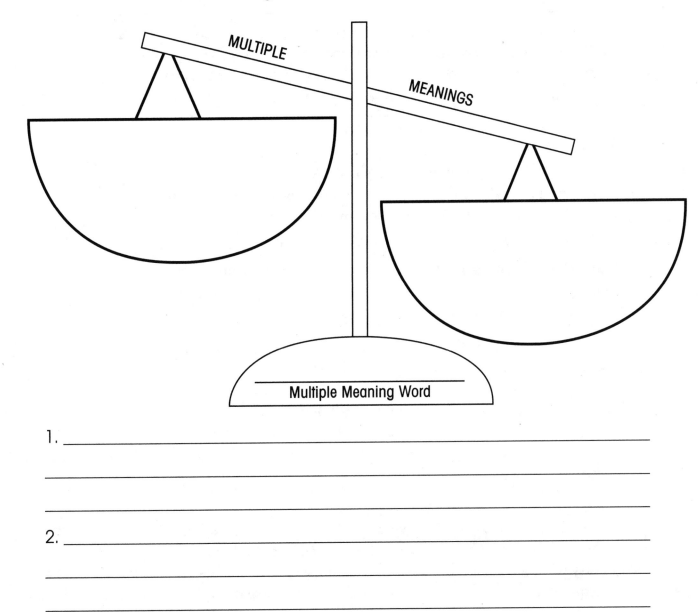

MULTIPLE

MEANINGS

Multiple Meaning Word

1. _____

_____

_____

2. _____

_____

_____

List any additional meanings for this word.

Visualization

Note About Visualization: Although visualization is an important comprehension strategy, remember children can only visualize concrete things and they may not be able to accurately represent their visualizations. So although helpful, visualizing is limited. Students may not be able to visualize the author's message or a story lesson, although they should always be thinking about it.

Pre-assessment

Read students two visually stimulating passages. On blank paper, have children draw what they see in their minds. Look for details and accuracy of information, taking into account artistic ability.

Visualization A   Students draw what they see in their minds as they are read to or when they read independently. There are hints to help them at the bottom of the page.

Visualization B   Students draw what they visualize. On this handout, there are places for some optional key words to supplement the visualization and aid in recall. Even though this is a visualization activity, the purpose is for students to remember what they read. The story message may not be part of the visualization.

Visualization C   Students draw visualizations or jot down key words, but here the visualization boxes are a bit more focused. Students should try to be aware of the sensory details presented as well as the story sequence. Again, the author's message may not be part of the visualization, but encourage students to think about it.

Whole-Class Book Chat

Have students share visually stimulating stories, highlighting the advantages of visualizing and noting its limitations. Students can share how visualizing techniques help.

Name: _____

Directions: As you read or listen to a story, draw what you see in your mind. Draw only the most important parts. Use your visualization to retell the story or recall key facts.

Title: _____

_____

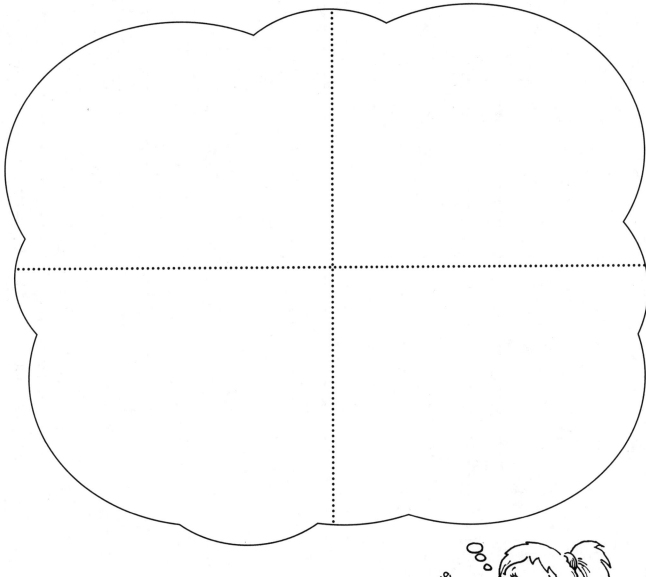

who   what   where   when   why   characters   setting   problem   solution   author's message

Name: _____

Directions: While reading or listening to a story, draw what you see in your mind. Write any key words on the lines. (It is hard to visualize some ideas, so the key words will help you recall important information.) Use your visualizations and key words to retell the story.

Title: _____

BEGINNING	MIDDLE	END

VISUALIZATION

B

Name: _____

Directions: Create a visualization based on what you read. Include key words and drawings to help you recall the story. Include sensory details and images. Be sure to think about the author's message even if it is not part of your visualization.

Title: _____

	**Beginning**	
	**Middle**	
	End	
	Author's Message	
	Key Words	

General/Specific

Please Note: These reproducibles can be used with fiction or nonfiction.

Pre-assessment

Present children with a general topic and ask them to provide two details. Then present them with four details and ask them to provide you with the topic.

General/Specific A   Fill in the title/topic and write the general statement related to a topic or story. Then have students use the general statement as a guide to write four related details. If it is a story, be sure the children know to go back into the text for supporting documentation. This is working whole to part. Option: Students can fill in the general statement and complete the remainder on their own.

General/Specific B   This handout is very similar to the first one, however, now the students will go from part to whole. Using details you provide, children will draw a conclusion and develop a general statement. Option: Students can provide the details and then generate the general statement.

General/Specific C   Students will determine the general statement and the specific details that support that statement. Students can then use their general statements and specific details to organize and write a paragraph.

Whole-Class Book Chat

Have students share their general statements and specific details related to their topics and stories. Students can begin to see the importance of this structure for their writing. Then try a common topic and create a general statement and specific detail statements together. Note the connection between these activities and planning a paragraph.

Name: _____

Directions: Use the general information provided or write your own general statement. Then write four related facts or details.

Title/Topic: _____

General Statement

|||||||||||||||||||||||||||||||||||||||||||||||||||||||||||||||||||||||||||||||||||||||

_____

_____

_____

_____

Related Fact/Detail

Related Fact/Detail

Related Fact/Detail

Related Fact/Detail

Name: _____

Directions: Use the specific details provided or write your own specific details. Then use the details to generate a related general statement.

Title/Topic: _____

Specific

Detail

Detail

Detail

General

_____
_____
_____
_____

Name: _____

Directions: In the star, write a general statement related to the topic.
In the four "bursts" write specific statements related to the general statement.

Title/Topic: _____

Specific

General

1.

2.

3.

4.

On a separate sheet of paper, compose a paragraph about the general topic. Plan your paragraph.
Use the general statement and specific details to support your writing.

Highlight: Nonfiction

Note: On each handout, students indicate whether they have prior knowledge of the topic. You can lead a discussion allowing students to share prior knowledge. Keep the discussion focused on the topic.

Pre-assessment

Present leveled nonfiction texts to students. Ask them to identify: *who*, *what*, *where*, *when*, and *why*. If applicable, have them note the main idea. Ask them to note any text features.

Nonfiction A   The teacher can choose the topic or leave it for the students to identify. The teacher will choose a specific heading or bold-faced word and write it in the provided box. Using the text, students will illustrate or create a labeled diagram related to the heading or key word. They can write key words below. Students will use the information gained to write a factual sentence.

Nonfiction B   Students will identify the topic and the source. Explain what "source" means and also note how to determine a reliable source. Be sure students understand how text features aid in comprehension. For this task, do not use font style as a text feature. Students will identify a specific text feature and note what information it provides. Then they will write a related statement and a related question for further review.

Nonfiction C   Students will identify: *who* or *what*, *where*, *when*, *why*, and *how* in the text. In addition, they will note two text features and the information that is provided by each. For this task, do not use font style as a text feature. This handout can be used in isolation or as an outline for a paragraph or summary to be completed on a separate piece of paper.

Whole-Class Book Chat

Students can work together and create class question-and-answer books either about a specific topic or about different topics. Students can then share their own pages. Encourage class discussion.

Name: _____

Directions: Identify the topic of the text if it is not already given. Note the provided heading or key word. Sketch a related illustration or label a diagram. Note any key words. Write a related fact.

Topic	Do you have any prior knowledge of this topic? ❏ Yes ❏ No

Heading or Key Word	

Sketch
• Illustrate
• Diagram

Key Words

_____   _____   _____

_____   _____   _____

Write a fact related to the information above.

_____

_____

_____

Name: _____

Directions: Identify the topic and the source. Choose two text features. Note what information the visuals provide. Write a related statement and a related question.

Topic	Do you have any prior knowledge of this topic? ❏ Yes ❏ No

Source

TEXT FEATURES page number if available	What information does the visual provide? Think about how it helps you understand.

Related Statement	_____ _____ _____

Related Question	_____ _____ _____

Name: _____

Directions: Write the topic and source. Write key words identifying text highlights using the guides below. Choose two text features and note the information provided by each visual. Use this information to write a summary or a paragraph on a separate paper.

Topic	Do you have any prior knowledge of this topic?
Source	❑ Yes ❑ No

Section of Text	

Who or What?	
Where?	
When?	
Why?	
How?	

TEXT FEATURES page number if available	What information does the visual provide? Think about how it helps you understand.

Appendix

Student Interest Inventory

1. Name: _____

2. Birthday: _____

3. Favorite subject or subjects:

   ☐ reading ☐ writing ☐ math ☐ science ☐ social studies

4. Why? _____
   _____

5. Least favorite subject: ☐ math ☐ science ☐ social studies

   ☐ reading ☐ writing

6. Why? _____
   _____

7. Are you able to work with some noise in the classroom or do you like it quiet?

   ☐ noise ☐ quiet

Parent Inventory

Child's name: _____

Parent/Guardian's name(s) _____

Best way to contact: _____

Note your child's academic and non-academic strengths.
_____
_____
_____

Note your child's academic and non-academic challenges.
_____
_____
_____

Does your child enjoy school? Explain. Try to provide specifics.
_____
_____
_____

Teacher Considerations

Take some time to consider these questions:

Do students like to work alone, with a partner, in a small group, or in a whole group? Be aware that it is not all or none. Some students are comfortable with multiple grouping formations.

Are your students creative? Would they like to prepare a skit, a song, a movie, or a cartoon to demonstrate their learning? Think beyond a poster.

Are your students ready for abstract material or are they able to handle concrete material more successfully?

Do the students prefer to learn material orally? Do they learn best using visuals? Are they kinesthetic learners?

Do the children have any attention issues?

What type of environment works best for the children?

What talents do the children bring to the task? (musical, artistic, mathematical, socially gifted)

116

Student Interest Inventory

1. Name: _____

2. Birthday: _____

3. Favorite subject or subjects:

   ❑ reading   ❑ writing   ❑ math   ❑ science   ❑ social studies

4. Why? _____

   _____

   _____

   _____

5. Least favorite subject:

   ❑ reading   ❑ writing   ❑ math   ❑ science   ❑ social studies

6. Why? _____

   _____

   _____

   _____

7. Are you able to work with some noise in the classroom or do you like it quiet?

   ❑ noise   ❑ quiet

8. Is it hard for you to concentrate on schoolwork?

    ❑ yes   ❑ no

9. Do you like to work _____: (You can choose more than one.)

    ❑ alone   ❑ with a partner   ❑ with a small group   ❑ whole class

10. When you work, do you like to: ❑ sit still   ❑ move around

11. I work slowly.   ❑ yes   ❑ no

12. When I am not in school, I like to: _____

    _____

    _____

    _____

    _____

13. My favorite thing is: _____

    _____

    _____

14. What else would you like your teacher to know about you?

    _____

    _____

    _____

    _____

15. On a separate sheet of paper, draw a picture of yourself doing
    something you enjoy.

Parent Inventory

Child's name: _____

Parent/Guardian's name(s) _____

_____

Best way to contact: _____

_____

Note your child's academic and non-academic strengths.

_____

_____

_____

_____

Note your child's academic and non-academic challenges.

_____

_____

_____

_____

Does your child enjoy school? Explain. Try to provide specifics.

_____

_____

_____

_____

How does your child deal with homework?

_____

_____

_____

What are his/her favorite subjects?

_____

_____

What are his/her least favorite subjects?

_____

_____

How do you think your child learns best?

_____

_____

What after-school activities does your child enjoy?

_____

_____

_____

Describe your child socially.

_____

_____

Supply any other information about your child.

_____

_____

_____

_____

Teacher Considerations

Take some time to consider these questions:

Do students like to work alone, with a partner, in a small group, or in a whole group? Be aware that it is not all or none. Some students are comfortable with multiple grouping formations.

Are your students creative? Would they like to prepare a skit, a song, a movie, or a cartoon to demonstrate their learning? Think beyond a poster.

Are your students ready for abstract material or are they able to handle concrete material more successfully?

Do the students prefer to learn material orally? Do they learn best using visuals? Are they kinesthetic learners?

Do the children have any attention issues?

What type of environment works best for the children?

What talents do the children bring to the task? (musical, artistic, mathematical, socially gifted)

Possible Alternative Assignments

Reminders for teachers:

Remember to make all directions and expectations clear. Review the assignments carefully with students. Check for understanding.

Be supportive. Provide children with all necessary materials and resources. Preview Internet sites that are appropriate. Guide them so they can find other resources on their own.

Be flexible. This list is just a start, a launching place. Students may have ideas of their own. Let them participate in the planning stage. Some of the best projects and ideas are student-generated.

Create flexible groups for these projects or allow students to sign up and choose their own. Some groups just naturally form based on student interests.

Have fun! This is where the children solidify learning.

Act out a scene or event.

Build with: blocks, clay, recyclables, wood, corrugated board, or any materials available.

Tape record a review or response to reading using various media.

Write an original poem. Illustrate it.

Design and conduct an interview.

Create a video.

Write an alphabet book.

Create an art gallery.

Role play an event or scenario from a book or real life.

Choose an important topic. Debate an issue.

Create a class book.

Make a game.

Be the teacher. Teach a lesson.

Sing and/or write a song.

Take photographs. Share and/or write about them.

Write a story, book, article, or newspaper.

Thumbnails of Sample Pages

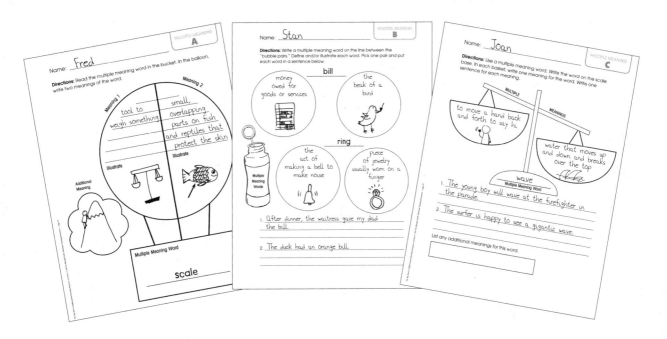

Traits (pages 15–17)

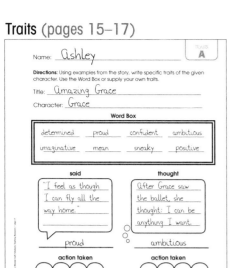

Name: Ashley

TRAITS A

Directions: Using examples from the story, write specific traits of the given character. Use the Word Box or supply your own traits.

Title: Amazing Grace

Character: Grace

Word Box

determined	proud	confident	ambitious
imaginative	mean	sneaky	positive

said
"I feel as though I can fly all the way home."

proud

thought
After Grace saw the ballet, she thought: I can be anything I want.

ambitious

action taken
Grace acted out adventure stories. She played all the parts herself.

imaginative

action taken
Grace practiced for the audition. She acted like Peter Pan and knew what to say.

confident

Name: Marco

TRAITS B

Directions: Choose a character. Identify three character traits. Provide specific text-based evidence to support your choices. In each circle, decide if you think the trait is a positive trait (+) or a negative trait (–).

- thinks
- says
- feels
- does
- travels

Title: Amos and Boris

Character: Amos, the mouse

Traits	Put the evidence in your own words.
ambitious (+)	Amos built a boat, studied navigation, loaded the boat with food and supplies, and set sail into the sea.
fearful (–)	Amos was alone and stranded in the sea and he was thinking very bad thoughts.
determined (+)	When Boris was stuck on the beach, Amos acted quickly to save Boris by bringing elephants to help.

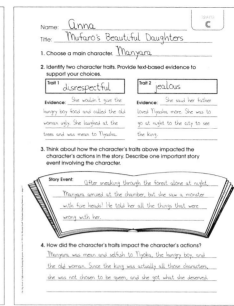

Name: Anna

TRAITS C

Title: Mufaro's Beautiful Daughters

1. Choose a main character. Manyara

2. Identify two character traits. Provide text-based evidence to support your choices.

Trait 1 disrespectful
Evidence: She wouldn't give the hungry boy food and called the old woman ugly. She laughed at the trees and was mean to Nyasha.

Trait 2 jealous
Evidence: She said her father loved Nyasha more. She was to go at night to the city to see the king.

3. Think about how the character's traits above impacted the character's actions in the story. Describe one important story event involving the character.

Story Event: After sneaking through the forest alone at night, Manyara arrived at the chamber, but she saw a monster with five heads! He told her all the things that were wrong with her.

4. How did the character's traits impact the character's actions?
Manyara was mean and selfish to Nyoka, the hungry boy, and the old woman. Since the king was actually all those characters, she was not chosen to be queen, and she got what she deserved.

Prediction (pages 19–21)

Name: Sami

PREDICTION A

Directions: Choose three clues or details from the Clue Box to help you make a prediction and label each box below. Draw or write information in each box to help you make a prediction.

Title: Are You My Mother?

CLUE BOX
Check three clues/details to help you predict:
- ☑ title
- ☑ cover illustration
- ☐ prior knowledge
- ☑ illustration in story
- ☐ character actions
- ☐ other

Clue/Detail: title
Someone is looking for their mother because they are lost.

Clue/Detail: cover illustration

I wonder if the little bird is lost. I don't think the dog is her mother.

Clue/Detail: illustration in the story
I think the new baby gets lost.

Prediction: I think the story will be about a new baby bird who gets lost and she goes looking for her mother.

Name: Mahad

PREDICTION B

Directions: Gather information from the story, the title, the illustrations, and your own experiences. Make a prediction. Explain your thinking and provide evidence to support your prediction.

Title: Dr. DeSoto

Check one: ☐ before reading   ☑ during reading

PREDICTION
I think the sly fox will try to eat Dr. DeSoto and Mrs. DeSoto, but he won't be able to because they will trick the fox.

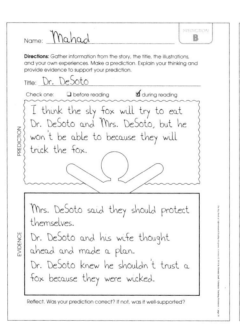

EVIDENCE
Mrs. DeSoto said they should protect themselves.
Dr. DeSoto and his wife thought ahead and made a plan.
Dr. DeSoto knew he shouldn't trust a fox because they were wicked.

Reflect. Was your prediction correct? If not, was it well-supported?

Name: Isabella

PREDICTION C

Directions: Gather story clues/details to make a prediction. Write the clues/details in the first box. Next use the story clues/details and your related knowledge to make a prediction. Then write an "I wonder..." statement as you prepare to read on. Repeat again later in the story.

Title: Silver Packages

Story Clues/Details
- Every child gets a silver package.
- For some children it's their only present.
- The rich man wants to give back.

Story Clues/Details
- Frankie opens his presents but doesn't get a doctor's kit.
- He wishes for a doctor's kit.

So I predict...
There will be one child who receives a special present in his or her silver package.

So I predict...
Frankie will get a doctor's kit.

I wonder... I wonder which child is on the cover and what present he will get.

I wonder... I wonder if Frankie will get a doctor's kit.

Characterization (pages 23–25)

CHARACTERIZATION A

Name: Quin

Directions: Identify a character. In the boxes, draw and write facts about the character. Use specific details from the story. Write a sentence describing the character.

Title: The Big Orange Splot

Looks Like
bald
big mustache

Says and Thinks
"My house is me and I am it." talks to his neighbors

Actions
paints his house like a rainbow
built a tower
planted palm trees
meets with his neighbors to talk about their dreams

Interests
swinging on his hammock
animals
steam shovels

Other Character Interactions
neighbors

Character: Mr. Plumbean
Sentence: Mr. Plumbean decorated his house to show his interests and dreams.

Name: Holly

CHARACTERIZATION B

Directions: Choose a character. Identify specific events or challenges involving that character. Write how the character responds to the specific event or challenge.

Title: Crickwing

Character Crickwing

Major Events and Challenges	Character Response
Crickwing was teased by the creatures in the forest.	Crickwing would stay away from the other creatures and try to get his food very late in the night.
The leafcutter ants saved Crickwing and he wanted to help save them from the army ants.	Crickwing and the leafcutter ants made an anteater sculpture. The army ants were scared away.

Name: Seamus

CHARACTERIZATION C

Directions: Choose a character. Identify one story event and the character's reaction to it. Write how the character's reaction impacts the rest of the story.

Title: Mirandy and Brother Wind

Character: Mirandy

Story Event
Orlinda made fun of Ezel and said she told Mirandy she would not dance with that clumsy boy.

Character's Reaction
Mirandy told Orlinda that she would dance with Ezel and they would win the cake.

How do the character's actions impact the rest of the story?
If Orlinda didn't make fun of Ezel then Mirandy would not have stood up for him and offered to be his partner. Since she accepted Ezel as a partner, she was able to win.

On a separate sheet of paper, describe the character in detail.
Think about...
- character traits
- motivations
- thoughts
- story events
- words spoken
- character actions
- feelings

Character Actions (pages 27–29)

Name: Daniel

Directions: Focus on one character. List three things the character did in the story. Illustrate one character action from your list. Write one telling sentence about the character.

Title: Fritz and the Beautiful Horses

Include details in your illustration.

Character: Fritz

1. Fritz watched the children on the horses.
2. Fritz crossed the river to get the children after the bridge broke.
3. Fritz carried all the children across the river to safety.

Sentence: After the bridge broke, Fritz was brave and strong and carried the children safely across the river.

Name: Craig

Directions: Choose a character. Identify one important action taken by that character. Fill in the small boxes to show the consequence of the action and how it impacts the story.

Title: Strega Nona

Big Anthony
Character

Character ACTION
Big Anthony took Strega Nona's pasta pot even when she told him not to touch it. He said the magic rhyme and it made pasta.

The pasta pot kept making pasta. It would not stop and it overflowed.
Consequence of Action

townspeople - the pasta flowed into town
Strega Nona - pasta filled her house
Other Characters Impacted by This Action

Based on the character's actions, draw a conclusion about the character.
Big Anthony was not a good listener and he was disrespectful because he did not follow Strega Nona's directions about the pasta pot.

Name: Stephen

Directions: Identify two important actions taken by one character. Then think about why the character took those actions. What was the MOTIVE?

Title: Lon Po Po
Character: Shang

CHARACTER ACTIONS	MOTIVE
Shang led Tao and Paotze to the gingko tree to eat the gingko nuts.	**What did the character want?** She wanted to get her sisters out of the house away from the wolf.
Shang told the wolf to get in the basket and she would pull it up the tree.	She wanted to kill the wolf so they would be safe.

Describe how the character's motives influenced his or her actions.
Shang's main motive was to keep herself and her sisters safe. Her actions needed to be clever in order to trick the wolf. First, she needed to get them out of the house and then she needed to get rid of the wolf.

Character Change (pages 31–33)

Name: Manuel

Directions: Note how the character changed over time. Use the Word Box words to help you.

Title: Jamaica Tag Along
Character: Jamaica

mean	excited	unfriendly	patient
kind	careless	helpful	bossy

Beginning
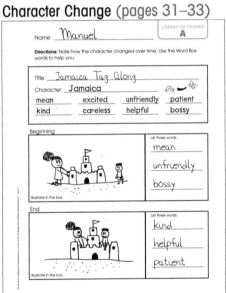
Illustrate in the box.

List three words.
mean
unfriendly
bossy

End
Illustrate in the box.

List three words.
kind
helpful
patient

Name: Shanika

Directions: Use key words to describe how the character acted at the beginning of the story and then at the end of the story. Explain how the character changed.

Title: The Recess Queen

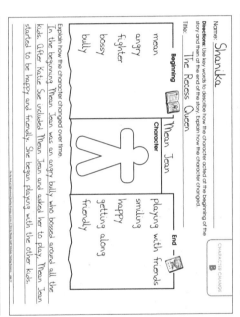

Character: Mean Jean

Beginning:
mean
angry
fighter
bossy
bully

End:
playing with friends
smiling
happy
getting along
friendly

Explain how the character changed over time.
In the beginning Mean Jean was an angry bully who bossed around all the kids. After Katie Sue included Mean Jean and asked her to play, Mean Jean started to be happy and friendly. She began playing with the other kids.

Name: Bianca

Directions: Think about how the character changed over time throughout the story.

Title: The Quiltmaker's Gift

WHO? the king

HOW did the character change?	WHY did the character change?
In the beginning the king was powerful and greedy. He always wanted presents and more presents. In the end the king learned it was better to give than receive.	The Quiltmaker agreed to make the king a quilt if he gave away all the things he owned. Little by little the king gave away all his things and that made him feel good inside.

Color.
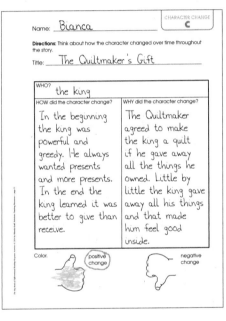
positive change

negative change

Main Idea (pages 35–37)

Name: Caia

Directions: Write the main idea in the flower. Write the title and details in the leaves. Cut out the leaves and paste them on the stem.

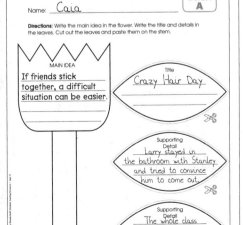

MAIN IDEA
If friends stick together, a difficult situation can be easier.

Title
Crazy Hair Day

Supporting Detail
Larry stayed in the bathroom with Stanley and tried to convince him to come out.

Supporting Detail
The whole class made their hair crazy for the picture.

Name: Lisa

Directions: Identify the topic, main idea, and supporting details.

Title/Headline: Little Gray Lighthouse and the Great Gray Bridge

Topic: teamwork/self-esteem

Main Idea: The little red lighthouse felt important because it helped keep the boats safe on the river.

Detail: The little lighthouse flashed its light and rang its bell to help direct the boats.

Detail: The great gray bridge told the lighthouse it was the master of the river and it was still needed to keep the boats safe.

Name: Duane

Directions: Identify the main idea and supporting details. List any key words. Answer the question below.

Title/Headline: Home Run

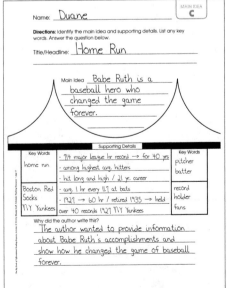

Main Idea: Babe Ruth is a baseball hero who changed the game forever.

Key Words	Supporting Details	Key Words
home run	- 714 major league hr record → for 40 yrs - among highest avg. hitters - hit long and high / 21 yr. career	pitcher batter
Boston Red Socks N.Y. Yankees	- avg. 1 hr every 11.7 at bats - 1927 → 60 hr / retired 1935 → held over 40 records 1927 N.Y. Yankees	record holder fans

Why did the author write this?
The author wanted to provide information about Babe Ruth's accomplishments and show how he changed the game of baseball forever.

Simile (pages 39–41)

Name: **Maurice** — SIMILE A

Directions: Read the simile. Illustrate what is being compared. Fill in the blanks below to support your drawing. In the oval, write what is common to both words being compared.

Simile: "He admired Mr. Drysdale who had a voice like a giant."
-Wilfrid Gordon McDonald Partridge

Illustrate. | Illustrate.

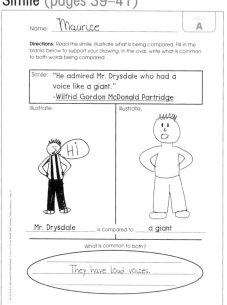

Mr. Drysdale   is compared to   a giant

What is common to both?

They have loud voices.

Name: **Lloyd** — SIMILE B

Directions: Read the simile or identify a simile. Write or illustrate the two things being compared in the middle box, write the common trait.

Simile: **as tall as a building**

Object 1

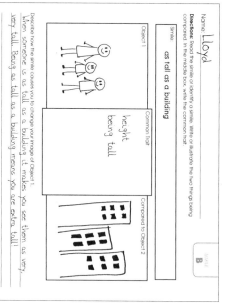

Common Trait: height being tall

Compared to Object 2

Describe how the simile causes you to change your image of Object 1. When someone is as tall as a building it makes you see them as very tall. Being as tall as a building means you are extra tall!

Name: **Tanya** — SIMILE C

Directions: Identify a simile. Illustrate the simile as it is used in the story. Write your responses to the questions below.

Title: **James and the Giant Peach**

simile

"She was like a great, white, soggy overboiled cabbage."

Illustrate the simile.

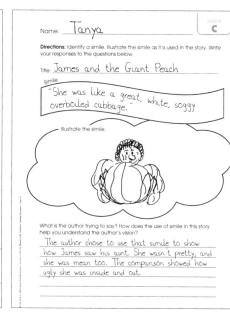

What is the author trying to say? How does the use of simile in this story help you understand the author's vision?

The author chose to use that simile to show how James saw his aunt. She wasn't pretty, and she was mean too. The comparison showed how ugly she was inside and out.

Retell (pages 43–45)

Name: **Celina** — RETELL A

Directions: Use pictures and words to help you retell the story.

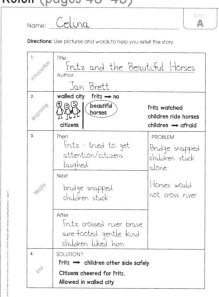

| 1. Introduction | Title: Fritz and the Beautiful Horses |
| | Author: Jan Brett |

2. Beginning — walled city Fritz → no / beautiful horses / citizens — fritz watched children ride horses / children → afraid

3. Middle	Then Fritz - tried to get attention/citizens laughed	PROBLEM Bridge snapped children stuck alone
	Next bridge snapped children stuck	Horses would not cross river
	After Fritz crossed river brave sure-footed gentle kind children liked him

4. End — SOLUTION? Fritz → children other side safely / Citizens cheered for Fritz. / Allowed in walled city

---

Name: **Kyle** — RETELL B

Directions: Make notes to help you retell the story aloud. Use key words, important phrases, and pictures. Decide the author's message.

Title: **Sylvester and the Magic Pebble**

Beginning
• Characters
• Setting

Sylvester Duncan Mom Dad
pebbles → special red pebble
wish came true - rain stop
must hold pebble - lucky

Middle
• Story events

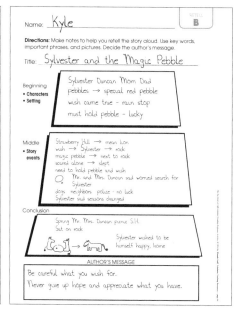

Strawberry Hill → mean lion
wish → Sylvester → rock
magic pebble → next to rock
scared alone → slept
need to hold pebble and wish
Mr. and Mrs. Duncan sad worried search for Sylvester
dogs neighbors police - no luck
Sylvester sad seasons changed

Conclusion

Spring Mr. Mrs. Duncan picnic S.H.
Sat on rock
Sylvester wished to be himself happy, home

AUTHOR'S MESSAGE

Be careful what you wish for.
Never give up hope and appreciate what you have.

Name: **Amy** — RETELL C

Directions: Use key words to walk down "Story Lane." Retell the story aloud. Answer the question below.

Title: **Frindle**

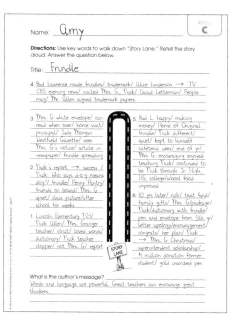

4. Bud Lawrence made frindles/ trademark/ Alice Lunderson → TV CBS evening news/ visited Mrs. G, Nick/ David Letterman/ People mag/ Mr. Allen signed trademark papers

3. Mrs. G white envelope/ can read when over/ home visit/ principal Judy Morgan/ Westfield Gazette/ sees Mrs. G's notice/ article in newspaper/ frindle spreading

2. Nick's report → success/ Nick: who says d-o-g means dog?/ frindle/ Penny Pantry/ friends on board/ Mrs. G upset/ class picture/after school for weeks

1. Lincoln elementary NH/ Nick Allen/ Mrs. Granger teacher/ strict/ loved words/ dictionary/ Nick teacher stopper/ not Mrs. G/

5. Bud L. happy/ making money/ Home of Original frindle/ Nick different/ quiet/ kept to himself cafeteria idea/ end of yr/ Mrs. G encouraging enjoyed teaching, Nick/ continued to be Nick through Jr. High, HS, college/school food improved

6. 10 yrs later/ rich/ trust fund/ family gifts/ Mrs. G/package/ Nick/dictionary with frindle/ pen and envelope from 5th gr/ letter apology/encouragement/ congrats/ her plan/ Nick → Mrs. G Christmas/ superintendent scholarship/ $1 million donation former student/ gold inscribed pen

STORY LANE

What is the author's message?
Words and language are powerful. Great teachers can encourage great thinkers.

Conflict (pages 47–49)

Name: **Meredith** — CONFLICT A

Directions: Answer the questions below. Write key words or sentences. Draw pictures and add labels.

Title: **Ruby the Copycat**

| What is the problem? | Who are the characters involved? |
| Ruby keeps copying Angela. | Ruby, Angela |

| Ruby | CONFLICT VS. | Angela |

| How was the problem solved? | Identify any other conflicts in the story. |
| Miss Hart spoke to Ruby. Miss Hart asked Ruby what she did over the weekend. Ruby showed everyone how she hopped. She was an amazing hopper. The class did the Ruby hop. | Ruby vs. Miss Hart. Ruby copied Miss Hart also. |

Name: **Ladonna** — CONFLICT B

Directions: Identify the conflict. Think about what the author wanted to say through this story conflict.

Title: **Peppe the Lamplighter**

| What is the problem? Use specific details from the story. | How is the problem solved? Use specific details from the story. |
| Peppe's father was not happy with Peppe's job as a lamplighter. He told him he wouldn't amount to anything. He wouldn't look at Peppe because he was ashamed. One night, Peppe didn't light the lamps and Assunta was missing. | Peppe's father was upset that Assunta was missing. He told Peppe to light the lamps. His father finally told Peppe his job as a lamplighter was important and he was proud of him. Peppe lit the lamps proudly and he found Assunta safe. |

What did the characters learn?
Peppe learned that his job was important. He helped keep people safe. Peppe's father learned to be proud of his son and he appreciated the job he did.

Name: **Robyn** — CONFLICT C

Title: **The Family Under the Bridge**

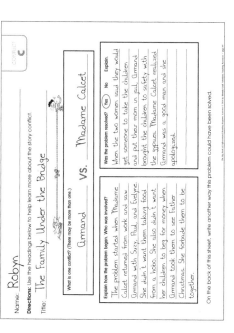

What is one conflict? (There may be more than one.)
Armand VS. **Madame Calcet**

Was the problem resolved? Yes No   Explain.

When the two women said they would get someone to take the children and put their mom in jail, Armand brought the children to safety. Madame Calcet realized the gypsies. Madame Calcet realized Armand was a good man and she apologized.

Explain how the problem began. Who was involved?
The problem started when Madame Calcet returned from work and saw Armand with Suzy, Paul, and Evelyne. She didn't want them taking food from a hobo. She also didn't want her children to beg for money when Armand took them to see father Christmas. She forbade them to be together.

On the back of this sheet, write another way this problem could have been solved.

Fact and Opinion (pages 51–53)

Name: Donna

Directions: Think about the story or article. Read the facts below. Choose two correct facts and paste them in the dish. Then write your opinions about the topic in the three scoops.

Title/Topic: Caps for Sale

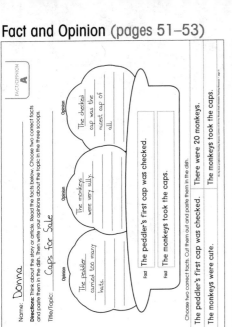

Opinion: The checked cap was the nicest cap of all

Opinion: The monkeys were very silly.

Opinion: The peddler carried too many hats.

fact | The peddler's first cap was checked.
fact | The monkeys took the caps.

Choose two correct facts. Cut them out and paste them in the dish.

The peddler's first cap was checked. | There were 20 monkeys.
The monkeys took the caps. | The monkeys were cute.

Name: Allison

Directions: Choose a topic if one is not provided. Next to the ruler write facts about the topic. Then next to the paintbrush write your opinion about the same subject. Support your opinion and tell why you feel that way.

Topic: character: Natasha

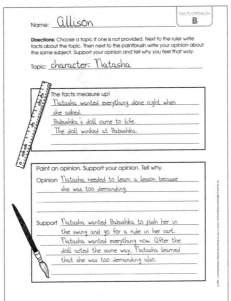

The facts measure up!
Natasha wanted everything done right when she asked.
Babushka's doll came to life.
The doll winked at Babushka.

Paint an opinion. Support your opinion. Tell why.

Opinion: Natasha needed to learn a lesson because she was too demanding.

Support: Natasha wanted Babushka to push her in the swing and go for a ride in her cart. Natasha wanted everything now. After the doll acted the same way, Natasha learned that she was too demanding also.

Name: Leslie

Directions: Read the opinion in Box A. Decide if you agree or disagree and check the correct box. Defend your response with factual information. If you write your own opinion, leave the ticket blank.

Box A

In The True Story of the Three Little Pigs, Alexander T. Wolf is not telling the truth.

☑ agree
☐ disagree

Defend your opinion. Use facts to support your opinion.

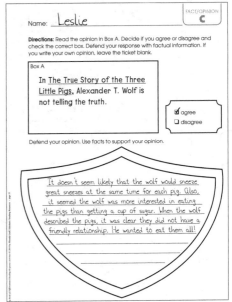

It doesn't seem likely that the wolf would sneeze great sneezes at the same time for each pig. Also, it seemed the wolf was more interested in eating the pigs than getting a cup of sugar. When the wolf described the pigs, it was clear they did not have a friendly relationship. He wanted to eat them all!

Compare and Contrast (pages 55–57)

Name: Yolanda

Directions: Compare and contrast. In the apples, use key words to note the similarities. In the pear and orange, use key words to note the differences. Then write one sentence for the similarities and one sentence for the differences.

COMPARE AND CONTRAST

Elmer and the other elephants

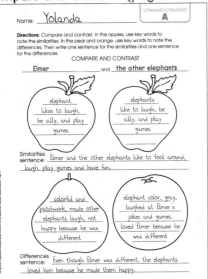

elephant likes to laugh, be silly, and play games

elephants like to laugh, be silly, and play games

Similarities sentence: Elmer and the other elephants like to fool around, laugh, play games and have fun.

colorful and patchwork, made other elephants laugh, not happy because he was different

elephant color, gray, laughed at Elmer's jokes and games, loved Elmer because he was different

Differences sentence: Even though Elmer was different, the elephants loved him because he made them happy.

Name: Enrique

Directions: Focus on the story element provided. Compare and contrast using two different texts.

Focus:

characters: Leo the Lion, Rainbow Fish

Title of Book 1: How Leo Learned to Be King

Title of Book 2: The Rainbow Fish

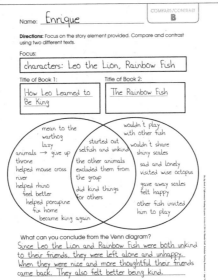

mean to the warthog
lazy
animals → give up throne
helped mouse cross river
helped rhino feel better
helped porcupine fix home
became king again

started out selfish and unkind
the other animals excluded them from the group
did kind things for others

wouldn't play with other fish
wouldn't share shiny scales
sad and lonely
visited wise octopus
gave away scales
felt happy
other fish invited him to play

What can you conclude from the Venn diagram?
Since Leo the Lion and Rainbow Fish were both unkind to their friends, they were left alone and unhappy. When they were nice and more thoughtful their friends came back. They also felt better being kind.

Name: Clarence

Directions: Choose two characters from the same book. Use the chart below to focus on their attributes. Draw a conclusion based on their similarities and differences.

Title: The Tale of the Mandarin Ducks

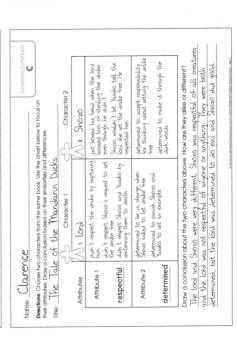

Attributes	Character 1 1. Lord	Character 2 2. Shozo
Attribute 1 respectful	didn't respect the drake by capturing him / didn't respect Shozo's request to set the drake free / didn't respect Shozo and Yasuko by sentencing them to death	got bowed his head when the lord accused him of stealing the drake even though he didn't / Shozo wouldn't let Yasuko tell the lord she set the drake free. He respected her.
Attribute 2 determined	determined to be in charge when Shozo asked to let drake free / determined to punish Shozo and Yasuko to set an example	determined to accept responsibility for thinking about setting the drake free / determined to make it through the dark woods

Draw a conclusion about the two characters above. How are they alike or different?
The Lord and Shozo were very different. Shozo was respectful of all creatures and the Lord was not respectful of anyone or anything. They were both determined, but the Lord was determined to do evil and Shozo did good.

Idiom (pages 59–61)

Name: Willa

Directions: Read the idiom. Draw the literal meaning. Then draw the true meaning. Write the meaning of the idiom in the box.

Idiom: ants in your pants

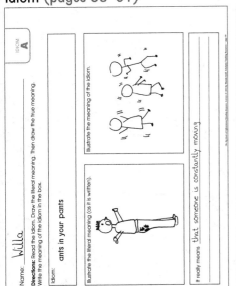

Illustrate the literal meaning (as it is written).

Illustrate the meaning of the idiom.

It really means: that someone is constantly moving

Name: Antonio

Directions: Read the idiom or choose an idiom and write its meaning. Illustrate the literal and actual meanings. Use the idiom in two sentences.

Idiom: in hot water

It means… being in big trouble

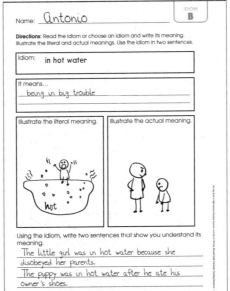

Illustrate the literal meaning. | Illustrate the actual meaning.

Using the idiom, write two sentences that show you understand its meaning.
The little girl was in hot water because she disobeyed her parents.
The puppy was in hot water after he ate his owner's shoes.

Name: Rose

Directions: Read the idiom or choose an idiom. Define it. Think about how it's used and answer the questions. Use the idiom in a sentence.

Idiom: every cloud has a silver lining

means: there is always something good even in a bad situation

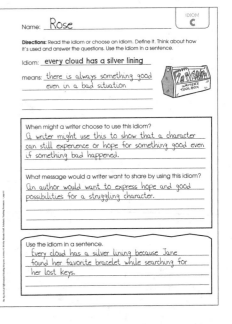

When might a writer choose to use this idiom?
A writer might use this to show that a character can still experience or hope for something good even if something bad happened.

What message would a writer want to share by using this idiom?
An author would want to express hope and good possibilities for a struggling character.

Use the idiom in a sentence.
Every cloud has a silver lining because Jane found her favorite bracelet while searching for her lost keys.

Setting (pages 63–65)

A

Name: **Ruth**

Directions: Identify the BEGINNING SETTING. List any key words that describe the setting. Then illustrate the setting. As the story progresses if the setting changes, complete the NEW SETTING portion the same way.

Title: **Corduroy**

BEGINNING SETTING	NEW SETTING
List key words:	List key words:
toy department	Lisa's apartment
big store	upstairs
shelf	
escalator	
day and night	
Illustrate the setting at the beginning of the story.	Illustrate another setting at a different point in the story.

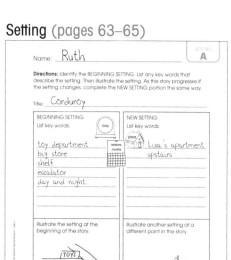

B

Title: **The Great Kapok Tree**

Name: **Sergio**

Directions: Describe the setting. Why is the setting important to the story?

- Setting
- Illustrate
- Use key words and phrases

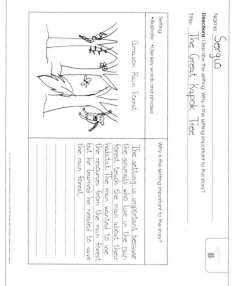

Amazon Rain Forest

Why is the setting important to the story?

The setting is important because the animals who live in the forest teach the man about their habitat. The man wanted to use the resources from the rain forest but he learned he needed to save the rain forest.

C

Name: **Terri**

Directions: Shed some light on the setting. Identify the setting in the light beam. Note if it changes. Then answer the setting-related questions.

Title: **The Butterfly**

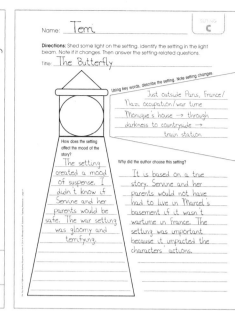

Using key words, describe the setting. Note setting changes.

Just outside Paris, France/ Nazi occupation/war time

Monique's house → through darkness to countryside → train station

How does the setting affect the mood of the story?

The setting created a mood of suspense. I didn't know if Sevrine and her parents would be safe. The war setting was gloomy and terrifying.

Why did the author choose this setting?

It is based on a true story. Sevrine and her parents would not have had to live in Marcel's basement if it wasn't wartime in France. The setting was important because it impacted the characters' actions.

Questioning (pages 67–69)

A

Name: **Callie**

Directions: Think about the story or text you are reading. Illustrate part of the text. Then write a related question. Choose another part of the text and repeat.

Title/Topic: **The Grouchy Ladybug**

Why does the ladybug want to fight all the animals?

How did the grouchy ladybug feel when it returned to the leaf at the end of the story? Explain why.

Try this! Write a telling sentence. Turn it into a question.

B

Title: **Just Plain Fancy**

Name: **Joe**

Directions: Using your knowledge of the story or article, pose questions for each question word. Make a prediction in the blank rainbow arches, make up your own questions.

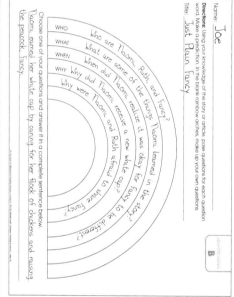

WHO — Who are Naomi, Ruth, and Fancy?

WHAT — What are some of the things Naomi realized in the story?

WHEN — When did Naomi receive a new white cap?

WHY — Why did Naomi and Ruth afraid to be different?

Why were Naomi and Ruth afraid?

Choose one of your questions and answer it in a complete sentence below.

Naomi earned her white cap by caring for her flock of chickens and raising the peacock, Fancy.

C

Name: **Emily**

Directions: Identify an event. Tell why it is important. Then "expand your thinking" and write a question about the event.

Title: **Sarah, Plain and Tall**

Event 1
Sarah writes a letter to Jacob saying she will come by train.

E·X·P·A·N·D your thinking
What made Sarah agree to come? What will keep her there for good?

Why is this event important?
Caleb, Anna, and Jacob were all hoping that Sarah would agree to come. They wanted a mother and wife. They were unsure, but hopeful.

Event 2
Papa, Caleb, Anna, and Sarah slid down the "hay dune".

E·X·P·A·N·D your thinking
Will Sarah be able to adjust to her new home and find things she loves enough to stay?

Why is this event important?
This is important because even though there wasn't a sand dune like Maine, there were fun things where they lived too.

Point of View and Perspective (pages 71–73)

A

Name: **Terence**

Directions: Identify who is telling the story. Decide if that person is in the story. There is room for two different books.

Title 1: **Through Grandpa's Eyes**

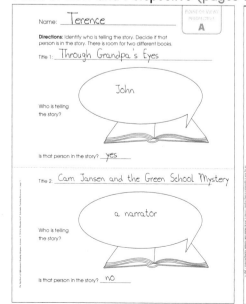

John

Who is telling the story?

Is that person in the story? **yes**

Title 2: **Cam Jansen and the Green School Mystery**

a narrator

Who is telling the story?

Is that person in the story? **no**

B

Title: **Enemy Pie**

Name: **Anthony**

Directions: Using a specific story event, note how each character's perspective.

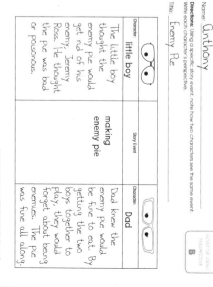

Character	Story event	Character
little boy		Dad
The little boy thought the enemy pie would get rid of his enemy, Jeremy Ross. He thought the pie was bad or poisonous.	making enemy pie	Dad knew the enemy pie would be fine to eat. By getting the two boys together to play, they would forget about being enemies. The pie was fine all along.

C

Name: **Misty**

Directions: Identify the point of view. Who is telling the story? Answer the questions below.

Title: **Maniac Magee**

Who is telling the story?
a narrator

Narrator?
Character?
Someone else?

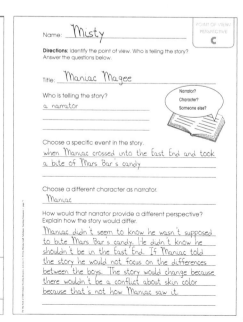

Choose a specific event in the story.
when Maniac crossed into the East End and took a bite of Mars Bar's candy

Choose a different character as narrator.
Maniac

How would that narrator provide a different perspective? Explain how the story would differ.
Maniac didn't seem to know he wasn't supposed to bite Mars Bar's candy. He didn't know he shouldn't be in the East End. If Maniac told the story he would not focus on the differences between the boys. The story would change because there wouldn't be a conflict about skin color because that's not how Maniac saw it.

Theme (pages 75–77)

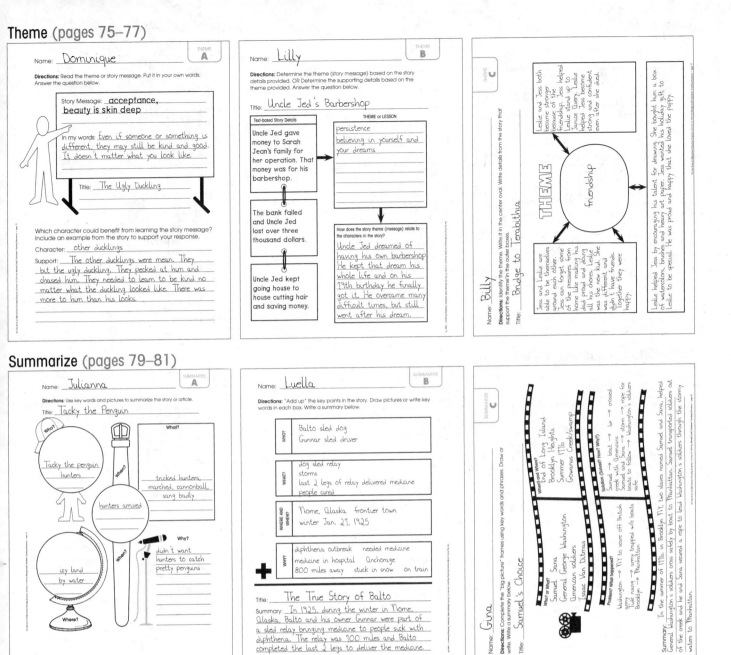

Name: Dominique — THEME A

Directions: Read the theme or story message. Put it in your own words. Answer the question below.

Story Message: acceptance, beauty is skin deep

In my words: Even if someone or something is different, they may still be kind and good. It doesn't matter what you look like.

Title: The Ugly Duckling

Which character could benefit from learning the story message? Include an example from the story to support your response.

Character: other ducklings

Support: The other ducklings were mean. They bit the ugly duckling. They pecked at him and chased him. They needed to learn to be kind no matter what the duckling looked like. There was more to him than his looks.

Name: Lilly — THEME B

Directions: Determine the theme (story message) based on the story details provided. OR Determine the supporting details based on the theme provided. Answer the question below.

Title: Uncle Jed's Barbershop

Text-based Story Details

Uncle Jed gave money to Sarah Jean's family for her operation. That money was for his barbershop.

The bank failed and Uncle Jed lost over three thousand dollars.

Uncle Jed kept going house to house cutting hair and saving money.

THEME or LESSON

persistence

believing in yourself and your dreams

How does the story theme (message) relate to the characters in the story?

Uncle Jed dreamed of having his own barbershop. He kept that dream his whole life and on his 79th birthday he finally got it. He overcame many difficult times, but still went after his dream.

Name: Billy — THEME C

Directions: Identify the theme. Write it in the center oval. Write details from the story that support the theme in the outer boxes.

Title: Bridge to Terabithia

THEME: friendship

- Jess and Leslie are able to be themselves around each other. Jess can forget some of the pressures from home like making his dad proud and doing all his chores. Leslie was the new kid. She was different and didn't have friends. Together they were happy.
- Leslie and Jess both helped each other because of the friendship. Jess helped Leslie stand up to Janice Avery. Leslie helped Jess become strong and confident even after she died.
- Leslie helped Jess by encouraging his talent for drawing. She bought him a box of watercolors, brushes and heavy art paper. Jess wanted his holiday gift to Leslie to be special. He was proud and happy that she loved the puppy.

Summarize (pages 79–81)

Name: Julianna — SUMMARIZE A

Directions: Use key words and pictures to summarize the story or article.

Title: Tacky the Penguin

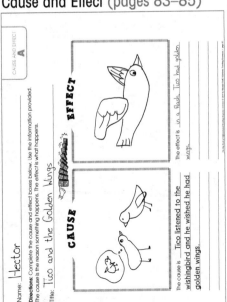

Who? Tacky the penguin, hunters

When? hunters arrived

What? tricked hunters, marched, cannonball, sang badly

Where? icy land by water

Why? didn't want hunters to catch pretty penguins

Name: Luella — SUMMARIZE B

Directions: "Add up" the key points in the story. Draw pictures or write key words in each box. Write a summary below.

WHO? Balto sled dog / Gunnar sled driver

WHAT? dog sled relay / storms / last 2 legs of relay delivered medicine / people cured

WHERE AND WHEN? Nome, Alaska frontier town / winter Jan. 27, 1925

WHY? diphtheria outbreak / needed medicine / medicine in hospital / Anchorage / 800 miles away / stuck in snow / on train

Title: The True Story of Balto

Summary: In 1925, during the winter in Nome, Alaska, Balto and his owner Gunnar were part of a sled relay bringing medicine to people sick with diphtheria. The relay was 700 miles and Balto completed the last 2 legs to deliver the medicine.

Name: Gina — SUMMARIZE C

Directions: Complete the story "big picture" frames using key words and phrases. Draw or write. Write a summary below.

Who or What? Samuel, Sara, General George Washington, American soldiers, Isaac Van Deemus

When and Where? End of Long Island, Brooklyn Heights, Summer 1776, Gowanus Creek/swamp

Problem? What happened? Washington → boat → Isaac → crossed creek with Americans, storm → rope for Samuel and Sara → Washington's soldiers boats to follow → Brooklyn → Manhattan

Solution (Solved? How? Who?) Washington → NY to scare off British army. Tide rises → army trapped w/o boats safe.

Title: Samuel's Choice

Summary: In the summer of 1776, in Brooklyn NY, two slaves named Samuel and Sara, helped General Washington's soldiers cross safely by boat to Manhattan. Samuel transported soldiers out of the creek and he and Sara secured a rope to lead Washington's soldiers through the stormy waters to Manhattan.

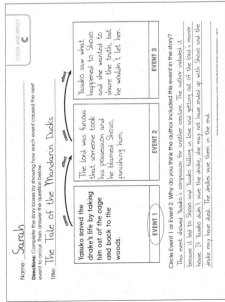

Cause and Effect (pages 83–85)

Name: Hector — CAUSE AND EFFECT A

Directions: Complete the cause and effect boxes below. Use the information provided. The cause is the reason something happens. The effect is what happens.

Title: Tico and the Golden Wings

CAUSE → EFFECT

The cause is Tico listened to the wishingbird and he had golden wings.

The effect is in a flash, Tico had golden wings.

Name: Wade — CAUSE AND EFFECT B

Directions: Complete the cause and effect boxes. Then answer the questions below.

Title: Sam, Bangs, and Moonshine

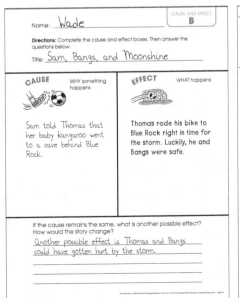

CAUSE WHY something happens

Sam told Thomas that her baby kangaroo went to a cave behind Blue Rock.

EFFECT WHAT happens

Thomas rode his bike to Blue Rock right in time for the storm. Luckily, he and Bangs were safe.

If the cause remains the same, what is another possible effect? How would the story change?

Another possible effect is Thomas and Bangs could have gotten hurt by the storm.

Name: Sarah — CAUSE AND EFFECT C

Directions: Complete the story boxes by showing how each event caused the next event to occur. Then answer the question below.

Title: The Tale of the Mandarin Ducks

EVENT 1: Yasuko saved the drake's life by taking him out of the cage and back to the woods.

EVENT 2: The lord was furious that someone took his possession and he blamed Shozo, punishing him.

EVENT 3: Yasuko saw what happened to Shozo and she wanted to share the truth, but he wouldn't let her.

Circle Event 1 or Event 2. Why do you think the author included this event in the story?

This event showed Yasuko's compassion for another creature. The author included it because it led to Shozo and Yasuko falling in love and getting out of the lord's manor house. If Yasuko didn't save the drake, she may not have ended up with Shozo and the drake may have died. The drakes saw them in the end.

Classify and Sort (pages 87–89)

A

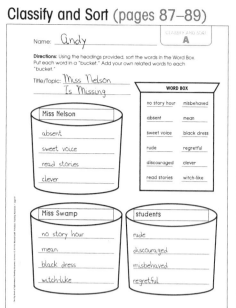

Name: Andy

Directions: Using the headings provided, sort the words in the Word Box. Put each word in a "bucket." Add your own related words to each "bucket."

Title/Topic: Miss Nelson Is Missing

WORD BOX

no story hour	misbehaved
absent	mean
sweet voice	black dress
rude	regretful
discouraged	clever
read stories	witch-like

Miss Nelson
- absent
- sweet voice
- read stories
- clever

Miss Swamp
- no story hour
- mean
- black dress
- witch-like

students
- rude
- discouraged
- misbehaved
- regretful

B

Name: Heather

Directions: Using the book or article presented, sort related words into the correct "bins." Give each group of words a heading. Create three headings. Then complete the prompts below.

Title/Topic: The Bears on Hemlock Mountain

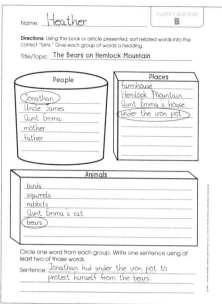

People
- Jonathan
- Uncle James
- Aunt Emma
- mother
- father

Places
- farmhouse
- Hemlock Mountain
- Aunt Emma's house
- under the iron pot

Animals
- birds
- squirrels
- rabbits
- Aunt Emma's cat
- bears

Circle one word from each group. Write one sentence using at least two of those words.

Sentence: Jonathan hid under the iron pot to protect himself from the bears.

C

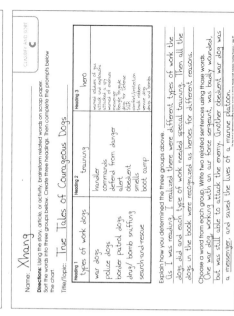

Name: Xhang

Directions: Using the story, article, or activity, brainstorm related words on scrap paper. Sort the words into three groups below. Create three headings. Then complete the prompts below the chart.

Title/Topic: True Tales of Courageous Dogs

Heading 1	Heading 2	Heading 3
types of work dogs	training	hero
war dogs	handler	warned soldiers of gas attack or explosion
police dogs	commands	attacked a spy
border patrol dogs	defend from danger	warned of ambush
drug/bomb sniffing	alert	messenger
search-and-rescue	obedient	found people trapped
	smells	dogs for defense
	boot camp	dogs for protection
		track robbers
		comfort/protection
		service dogs
		dogs used in war

Explain how you determined the three groups above. As I was reading, I realized there were different types of work the dogs did and each type of work needed special training. Then all the dogs in the book were recognized as heroes for different reasons.

Choose a word from each group. Write two related sentences using those words. One war dog, working with an air force sergeant, was badly wounded, but was still able to attack the enemy. Another obedient war dog was a messenger, and saved the lives of a marine platoon.

Interesting Language (pages 91–93)

A

Name: Thiago

Directions: Read the section of text in Box A below. Draw or write in your own words what you think the author wanted the reader to know. Underline any interesting words.

Title: The Relatives Came

BOX A

"But none of us thought about Virginia much. We were so busy hugging and eating and breathing together."

I think the author is saying…

Illustrate

Everyone was happy being together. The most important thing was that they could spend so much time as a family.

B

Name: Michael

Directions: Read the sections of text in the "Author's Words" boxes. Think about how the author chose certain words to convey a message or create a feeling. In your own words, write what the author wanted to convey.

Title: The Art of Miss Chew

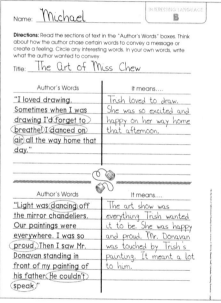

Author's Words	It means…
"I loved drawing. Sometimes when I was drawing I'd forget to breathe! I danced on air all the way home that day."	Trish loved to draw. She was so excited and happy on her way home that afternoon.

Author's Words	It means…
"Light was dancing off the mirror chandeliers. Our paintings were everywhere. I was so proud. Then I saw Mr. Donavan standing in front of my painting of his father. He couldn't speak."	The art show was everything Trish wanted it to be. She was happy and proud. Mr. Donavan was touched by Trish's painting. It meant a lot to him.

C

Name: Jessie

Directions: While reading, choose two interesting quotes. Look for exciting use of language, vivid imagery (mental pictures), and powerful words. Write the quote and then write why it attracted you. Think about what the author wanted the reader to think. Write your understanding of the quote.

Title: January's Snow

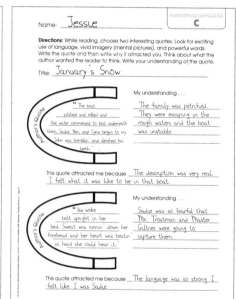

Author's Quote: "The boat pitched and rolled and the water commenced to boil underneath them. Sadie, Ben, and Cyrus began to cry. John was tremblin' and clenched his teeth."

My understanding… The family was petrified. They were escaping in the rough waters and the boat was unstable.

This quote attracted me because The description was very real. I felt what it was like to be in that boat.

Author's Quote: "She woke bolt upright in her bed. Sweat was runnin' down her forehead and her heart was beating so hard she could hear it."

My understanding… Sadie was so fearful that Mr. Trautman and Master Giltner were going to capture them.

This quote attracted me because The language was so strong I felt like I was Sadie.

Multiple Meaning Words (pages 95–97)

A

Name: Fred

Directions: Read the multiple meaning word in the bucket. In the balloon, write two meanings of the word.

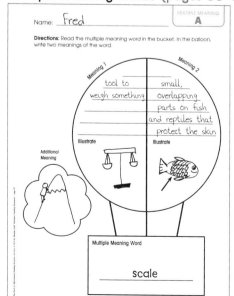

Meaning 1: tool to weigh something

Meaning 2: small, overlapping parts on fish and reptiles that protect the skin

Additional Meaning
Illustrate

Illustrate

Multiple Meaning Word
scale

B

Name: Stan

Directions: Write a multiple meaning word on the line between the "bubble pairs." Define and/or illustrate each word. Pick one pair and put each word in a sentence below.

bill
- money owed for goods or services
- the beak of a bird

Multiple Meaning Words

ring
- the act of making a bell to make noise
- piece of jewelry usually worn on a finger

1. After dinner, the waitress gave my dad the bill.

2. The duck had an orange bill.

C

Name: Joan

Directions: Use a multiple meaning word. Write the word on the scale base. In each basket, write one meaning for the word. Write one sentence for each meaning.

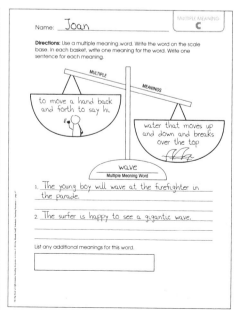

MULTIPLE MEANINGS

to move a hand back and forth to say hi

water that moves up and down and breaks over the top

wave
Multiple Meaning Word

1. The young boy will wave at the firefighter in the parade.

2. The surfer is happy to see a gigantic wave.

List any additional meanings for this word.

Visualization (pages 99–101)

Name: Edwin

Directions: As you read or listen to a story, draw what you see in your mind. Draw only the most important parts. Use your visualization to retell the story or recall key facts.

Title: Poppleton in Winter "The Sleigh Ride"

who what where when why characters setting problem solution author's message

---

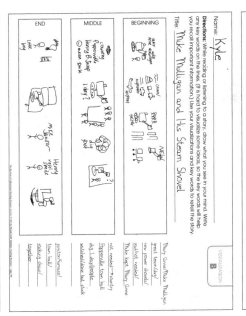

Name: Kyle

Title: Mike Mulligan and His Steam Shovel

BEGINNING | MIDDLE | END

Name: Miguel

Directions: Create a visualization based on what you read. Include key words and drawings to help you recall the story. Include sensory details and images. Be sure to think about the author's message even if it is not part of your visualization.

Title: Come On, Rain!

heat waves off tar patches gray clouds bunched and bulging trees sway glistening in our rain skin	**Beginning** extreme heat waiting for rain everyone waiting for rain Mamma Tessie clouds come
the smell of hot tar and garbage bullies the air rains coming Mamma turns to window and sniffs	**Middle** Tessie→Jackie Joyce's bathing suits Tessie makes tea→Mamma really hot→waiting rain Jackie comes over in our gets Liz, and Rosemary
sizzling like a hot potato needle sticks on phonograph squealing and whooping the streaming rain	**End** rain comes Tessie, Jackie, Liz and Rosemary play in the rain parents come out in rain undress – all laughing and dancing
dim, stuffy cave of her room slick with sweat sweat trickles down her neck breeze blows air cools	**Author's Message** importance of a new start enjoying life's simple things
aim a spoonful of sugar into my mouth we gulp down the rain	**Key Words** Come On, Rain! Ice-chilled parched sizzling breeze swollen broiling sky rain comes

---

General/Specific (pages 103–105)

Name: Jackie

Directions: Use the general information provided or write your own general statement. Then write four related facts or details.

(Title)/Topic: The Talking Eggs

General Statement
Blanche was a kind-hearted, thoughtful, respectful girl.

Related Fact/Detail
Blanche kept her promise not to laugh at anything she saw at the old woman's house.

Related Fact/Detail
Blanche lit fire as she was told/boiled bone

Related Fact/Detail
Blanche didn't stop or say anything when the old woman took off her head.

Related Fact/Detail
Blanche/chicken/house/ don't take me/eggs/ listened

Name: Kirk

Directions: Use the specific details provided or write your own specific details. Then use the details to generate a related general statement.

Title/Topic: Kamishibai Man

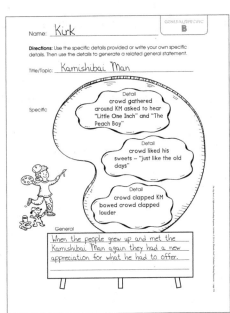

Specific

Detail crowd gathered around KM asked to hear "Little One Inch" and "The Peach Boy"

Detail crowd liked his sweets – "just like the old days"

Detail crowd clapped KM bowed crowd clapped louder

General
When the people grew up and met the Kamishibai Man again they had a new appreciation for what he had to offer.

Name: Vanessa

Directions: In the star, write a general statement related to the topic. In the four "bursts" write specific statements related to the general statement.

Title/Topic: The Junkyard Wonders

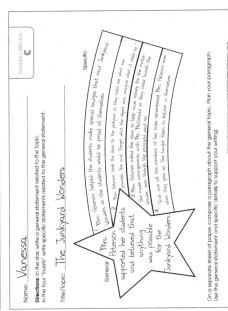

Specific

1. Mrs. Peterson helped the students make special badges that said Junkyard Wonders so the students would be proud of themselves.

2. Mrs. Peterson took the class to the junkyard so they could see what was possible. She said "Forget what the object was, imagine what it could be."

3. Mrs. Peterson asked the class to help raise money for the rocket She made arrangements with Mr. McDonald so they could launch the rocket, even though the principal said no.

4. Trish and all the members of her tribe remembered Mrs. Peterson, even when they grew up. She taught them to believe in themselves.

General
Mrs. Peterson supported her students and believed that anything was possible for the Junkyard Wonders.

On a separate sheet of paper, compose a paragraph about the general topic. Plan your paragraph. Use the general statement and specific details to support your writing.

Highlight: Nonfiction (pages 107–109)

Name: Clarissa

Directions: Identify the topic of the text if it is not already given. Note the provided heading or key word. Sketch a related illustration or label a diagram. Note any key words. Write a related fact.

Topic	Do you have any prior knowledge of this topic?
Weather	☑ Yes ☐ No

Heading or Key Word
Wind

Sketch / illustrate / diagram
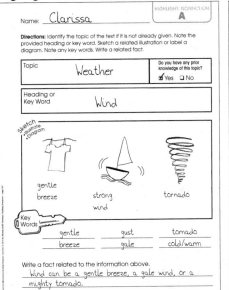
gentle breeze   strong wind   tornado

Key Words
gentle   gust   tornado
breeze   gale   cold/warm

Write a fact related to the information above.
Wind can be a gentle breeze, a gale wind, or a mighty tornado.

Name: Pavel

Directions: Identify the topic and the source. Choose two text features. Note what information the visuals provide. Write a related statement and a related question.

Topic	Do you have any prior knowledge of this topic?
Weather	☑ Yes ☐ No

Source
Tornadoes!

TEXT FEATURES page number if available	What information does the visual provide? Think about how it helps you understand.
illustrations pages 16-20	The illustrations show the extreme damage caused by tornadoes.
map p. 23	The maps of the US show Tornado Alley, from Texas to the Dakotas.
Related Statement	A tornado is so powerful it can blow off a roof, toss a train off the tracks, and flip a house upside down.
Related Question	Besides Tornado Alley, where else might a tornado touch down?

Name: Connie

Directions: Write the topic and source. Write key words identifying text highlights using the guides below. Choose two text features and note the information provided by each visual. Use this information to write a summary or a paragraph on a separate paper.

Topic	Weather/Hurricane Sandy	Do you have any prior knowledge of this topic?
Source		☑ Yes ☐ No

Section of Text	cover story, p. 2
Who or What?	survived Superstorm Sandy/Elizabeth Nies
Where?	Breezy Point, NY
When?	Oct. 29, 2012/a year later
Why?	family headed upstairs/bay overflowed
How?	2 months/grandfather's house

TEXT FEATURES page number if available	What information does the visual provide? Think about how it helps you understand.
map (inset) p. 2	The map highlights the area of the U.S. hit by Hurricane Sandy.
photograph and caption p. 2	The photograph shows that Breezy Point was destroyed from the hurricane. It shows how much damage the storm caused.

Bibliography

Boyles, N. (2012–2013). Closing in on Close Reading. *Educational Leadership.* Vol, 70 No. 4, pp 36–41.

Hochman, J. (2009). *Teaching Basic Writing Skills: Strategies for Effective Expository Writing Instruction.* Cambium Learning Sopris West.

Tomlinson, C.A. (2001). *How to Differentiate Instruction in Mixed Ability Classrooms,* 2nd Edition. ASCD: Alexandria VA.

Tomlinson, C.A. & Imbeau, M. (2010). *Leading and Managing a Differentiated Classroom.* ASCD: Alexandria VA.